Judi is a living example that it is possible to find your life's purpose and passion. In this book she shares the tools she used to achieve success and happiness. I recommend it for everyone trying to create the lives they desire.

— MONTEL WILLIAMS, TV HOST
THE MONTEL WILLIAMS SHOW

You are More Than Enough *lifts you up to believe in yourself. Judi Moreo has such great tips and stories that before you know it you have sailed right through this friendly, encouraging book. If you have the slightest thought that you aren't enough of what you must be, do, or have, then you must read Judi's latest book.*

— CHERIE CARTER-SCOTT, PhD, AUTHOR
NEGAHOLICS: HOW TO OVERCOME NEGATIVITY AND TURN YOUR LIFE AROUND;
IF SUCCESS IS A GAME, THESE ARE THE RULES; AND
IF LIFE IS A GAME, THESE ARE THE RULES

Judi's latest book is an indispensable tool for anyone wanting to make a success of her life. She brings her topic alive, giving great real life examples of people who have succeeded through living their lives with passion and belief in themselves.

— MARY MONAHAN, AUTHOR
REMEMBER ME?

When I read Judi's book, I couldn't stop. She has an extraordinary way of communicating. Combine that with her world-class sophistication, and strategies for positive living, and you have the owners' manual for success. This book will lift up anyone who reads it!

— DR. CASEY MCNEAL, AUTHOR
BUILDING RELATIONSHIPS: EFFECTIVE
STRATEGIES FOR HOW TO WORK WITH PEOPLE

If you've ever felt that something is missing from your life, but you don't know what it is or how to get it, read this book. Judi Moreo knows that "You Are More Than Enough" and she will show you how to claim your power, find your purpose, and embrace it with passion.

— ROBIN JAY, AUTHOR
THE ART OF THE BUSINESS LUNCH ~ BUILDING RELATIONSHIPS BETWEEN 12 AND 2
PRESIDENT OF THE LAS VEGAS CONVENTION SPEAKERS BUREAU

In equal measure, Judi Moreo challenges, inspires, and encourages. Sometimes she pulls you along, sometimes she pushes and sometimes she just cheers you on - but she always makes sure that you do it yourself.

— Ruth St. Pierre
Creative Business Resources, Inc.

I enjoyed what I read very much. I like the way Judi tells stories, and how she creates a solution to many of the issues pointed out in those stories. I know many people will benefit from her straightforward advice.

— Linda Armstrong Kelly, Professional Speaker and Author
Mother of Lance Armstrong

I loved the book! Judi Moreo reveals the secret of amazingly successful people and how they create their own opportunities and happiness. Full of powerful tools and strategies, this book is a comprehensive yet easy-to-follow guide on creating the life you desire.

— Allison Blankenship
Founder, Life Divas, Inc.

As an architect, I know how important a blueprint is to the process of creating a beautiful building. Judi's powerful book is like a set of construction documents for creating a beautiful life. Men should read it as well.

— Wallace Palmer, Architect

Ms. Moreo motivates you to tap into your innate potential to create new and exciting realities. A must read for anyone who wants to take charge of her life from the inside out!

— Sheryl Benzon, M. A., M.F.T.
President, Ventures in Excellence, Inc.

This guide for women provides a simple, yet profound look at how we, as women, are designed and then why we become who we ultimately become. This book is a "must have" for the young professional starting out, the housewife who has lost herself in her family, and the middle-aged woman who seems to have everything, but is still searching for passion and purpose.

— Dr. Kimberly Ventus-Darks
Human Whirlwind with Passion and Wisdom

You Are
More Than
Enough

Stephens Press · Las Vegas, Nevada

You Are More Than Enough

Every Woman's Guide To

Purpose, Passion & Power

Judi Moreo

Editor: Jami Carpenter
Art Director: Sue Campbell
Publication Coordinator: Stacey Fott

Cataloging in Publication.
Moreo, Judi.
You are more than enough: every woman's guide to purpose, passion and power
/ Judi Moreo.
256 p. ; 23 cm.
Summary: Includes techniques, ideas, and exercises to guide women to evalu-
ate and improve their lives.
ISBN: 1-932173-72-2
ISBN-13: 978-1-932173-72-7
1. Self-realization in women. 2. Women—Psychology. 3. Psychology, Applied.
I. Title.
158.1 dc22   2007
2006932475

Second Printing — June 2007

 STEPHENS PRESS, LLC
A Stephens Media Company

Post Office Box 1600
Las Vegas, NV 89125-1600
www.stephenspress.com

Printed in Hong Kong

In memory of

my wonderful parents

Daisy and Paul Shropshire

For all you were and all you did;

for giving me unconditional love

and

teaching me to live with purpose and passion.

Contents

Foreword

Readers, you are in for a treat. The book you are about to read is atypical for its genre; its advice is practical, doable, and might actually change your life. In a society increasingly populated by so-called life coaches and motivational speakers, author Judi Moreo stands out as a woman of sincere passion and sensible intelligence. She won't have you chanting mantras or obsessing over childhood events. Instead, Judi presents herself as an experienced, triumphant adult who is willing to divulge her "secret." She shares the valuable lessons acquired on her personal road to success, and the advice is truly beneficial. If you are in any way *tolerating* your life instead of *creating* your life, Judi Moreo is the mentor for you.

I first met Judi Moreo about forty years ago. I had enrolled my young daughter in a deportment class, hoping that she would learn the poise and etiquette I sometimes feared I lacked. The instructor was Judi Moreo. She taught my daughter grace, carriage, communication, and positive choices. Simultaneously (and probably unintentionally), she taught me about self-confidence and inner beauty. Judi became my friend for life.

Over the past four decades, I have watched Judi transform herself into a highly successful, powerful, and beloved woman. I can assure you it didn't come easily. Judi is a real woman with real struggles; her life isn't showered in pixie dust. Judi works, struggles, and perseveres. But she has learned how to make things happen for herself, and she is willing to share her knowledge with you. This is advice you can't turn down!

During my many years with a professional women's service organization, Soroptimist International, I have met countless talented, intelligent women who inexplicably believe themselves inferior or stuck. It is astonishing how few of us are genuinely excited about our lives. That is why I'm so thrilled about Judi's decision to write *You Are More Than Enough*. This book is necessary, and I truly believe Judi is the best writer for the job.

Across the globe are many women whose lives are testimony to Judi's personal and professional success. She is an amazing public speaker; her programs and training sessions provide positive opportunities for more complete inner knowledge and personal fulfillment. If you approach this book with an open mind — if you are prepared to transform the ideas into actions — I am confident that you will reap the rewards of Judi's amazing gift, and come to recognize the success story that lies within you.

— LOIS SAGEL, INTERNATIONAL PROGRAMME DIRECTOR
SOROPTIMIST INTERNATIONAL
"A GLOBAL VOICE FOR WOMEN"

Preface

Dear Reader:

Did you think you would be more successful by now? Do you want something, but don't know what it is? Are you struggling with finding your life purpose? Are you disappointed and discouraged with where you are or where you seem to be headed? Do you feel like you were created for something more, but you just don't know what?

If so, you aren't alone. This past year as I traveled across the country, speaking each day to audiences of 50 to 3000 people, I asked those questions. After each question, more than 75 percent of the audience raised their hands.

Why do so many people feel like they just aren't enough? Why do you feel this way? What do you need to do differently? This book will help you decide what you want to achieve in order to accomplish that "something more" you know is your destiny. It will help you determine what you can change in order to live a more fulfilling life . . . a life of purpose, passion, and power.

You may be thinking that you've tried before to make a fresh start and it didn't work. Perhaps that time you didn't have the necessary tools to make the changes. This time will be different. Throughout this book, I will be sharing tools and techniques with you that I used which helped me immensely in my journey to become the person I knew I could be. I understood I had purpose and I felt there was a passion deep within me that would lead me to a place of peace where I could know who I was and what I could achieve. I had to learn to unleash that passion in order to discover and use my personal power to fulfill my life dreams.

When I was in high school, my dream was to write a life-changing book. It's taken many years to be able to do it. I had to live life in order to write about it. In writing this book and sharing my personal stories, it was my goal to make your life a little easier, a bit more successful, and a great deal more satisfying. It is my hope that in this book you will find the support and encouragement that will assist you in becoming the person you know you can be. In fulfilling your purpose, you will have fulfilled mine as well. If the information in this book helps even one person create a more successful life, it will have been worth the writing.

—Judi Moreo

Acknowledgements

To **Carolyn Hayes Uber**, for being the best publisher ever; I like, respect, appreciate, and admire her. To **Thom Pruitt** for believing in my idea and bringing it to my publisher's attention; **Jami Carpenter**, my editor, for making my product even better than I wrote it; **Bob Walker**, who guided and supported me throughout the process of writing this book; **Charlotte Foust**, who wrote the affirmations in this book, along with brainstorming, sharing ideas, and supporting me through the rough moments; **Robin Jay**, for her unwavering support, editing, and suggestions. **Fiona Carmichael**, my business partner and forever friend; **Carol Scott**, for suggesting the title of the book; **Dana Anderson**, of Allen Photography, for the cover photograph; **Sue Campbell**, for the book design, **Stacey Fott**, for all her coordinating efforts; **Elfriedi Abbe**, for teaching me how to write a query letter that sells; **Jo Wilkins**, **Greg Kompes**, and the **Henderson Writers' Group**, for putting on a fabulous conference and providing the opportunity to meet Thom Pruitt and Carolyn Hayes Uber; **Dan Poynter**, for providing guidance in the writing process; my niece, **Morgan Pryor**, for spending her holidays answering my phone so I could get the book written; my sisters, **Lois Miller**, **Betty Stanley**, **Wanda Buchanan**, and my brother, **Wayne Gage**, for always believing in me and standing by me; my mentors, **Harry Yagoda**, **Millie Rubin**, **Ray Paglia**, **Lois Sagel**, **Roz Caldwell**, **Phyllis Kirkwood**, **Florence McClure**, **Geneva Douglas**, and **Bernadine Schneider**, for sharing their wisdom; my special friends, **Lynette Chappell**, **Lowell Lampe**, **Jerry Traylor**, **Sherial Bratcher**, **Cheri Carter-Scott**, **Ron DiCenzo**, **Lucy Belt**, **Mary Monahan**, **Elmiree Farr Walter**, **Jesse Ferrell**, **Ruth St. Pierre**, **Lisa Walker**, **Wallace Palmer**, **Jody Sneag**, **Brenda Sneag**, **Casey McNeil**, **Allison Blankenship**, **Kimberly Ventus-Darks**, **Tammy Wilson**, **Catherine Schelling**, **Joe Gilliam**, **Candy Whirley**, **Jill Wesley**, **Courtney Anderson**, **Sharon Spano**, **Trish Jeske**, **Pam Birchfield**, **Sue Bracksieck**, **Charlie Carter**, **Marie Pretorius**, **Sheryl Benzon**, **Pam Royle**, **Dick Davis**, **Adam**

Elliott, **Ron Willingham**, **Pam West**, and **Ellen Ackerman**, as well as **Atiq Nasib** and **Lorrie Nasib**, **John Futrell**, **Merle Whale**, **Jim Jackson**, **Peter Pizor**, **Kathy Jones**, **Anita Paul-Johnson**, **Cam Usher**, **Vimmi Kruger**, **Jerry Broach**, **Eriq Cook**, **Dave Carter**, **Alice Fessenden**, **Robert Forsythe**, **Micki Holliday**, **Julie Neil**. **Vicky Newell**, **Cheryl Smith**, and **Chuck Wagner** for their support.

Also, thank you to **Melanie McLaughlin**, **Debbie Lefever**, **Elizabeth Julia Stoumen**, **Jim Grigsby**, **Shirley Cheng**, **Melanie Camp**, **Tami Belt**, **Mary Maher**, **Gia DiMuzio**, **Steve Wilson**, **Barry Maher**, **Roxanne Roy**, **Donna Goertz**, **Janice Bates**, **Laurette A. Davis**, **Mike Benjamin**, **Claudia James**, **Cheri Burback**, **Suzanne Frisse**, **Naomi Ross**, **Heather Lusky**, **Kathleen Randall**, **Jeanette Kettle**, **Stacey Kannenberg**, **Derrick Hurd**, and **Cattel** for their communication and support.

Introduction

How to Use This Book

You have to be ready to read this book. This is not a "feel good" book. This is a "be good" book. I will even go so far as to say it's a "be excellent" book. You will go through a whole range of emotions. You may cry. You may laugh. You may even get angry. To get the most out of this book, you will need to be open, willing, and prepared to think about what you read and put into practice the techniques and skills I will share with you. I know they work! I use them.

Many self-help books give you "what if" generalized scenarios and airy, fairy solutions that are meaningless. This book is not about sitting around in a circle holding hands and singing campfire songs. It's about the mechanics of living in the real world; it's the nuts and bolts of life. I give you examples of real people I know or have known and how they solved problems or dealt with challenges. Stories help us to see that other people have gone through some of the same experiences we have. Experience is a wise teacher . . . whether it is our own or someone else's. This book shows you how to have a better, more successful, meaningful life. It shows you how to get the world to recognize your purpose, passion, and power.

Changing your life is a process. From time to time, you may have to put this book down and really think about what you've read. You may want to stop reading altogether and put some of the techniques into action before you continue. At the end of each chapter, I give you a skill to practice and an affirmation. If you are serious about finding your purpose, passion, and power, do the exercise right away and read the affirmation aloud twice a day every day for a minimum of twenty-one days.

I know from experience the right book can change your life. Use the ideas, techniques, and exercises in this book and you will dramatically improve your life. If you take this information to heart and make it a personal development course, you will soon find yourself getting the things you want, associating with the people you would like to have in your life, achieving the success you desire, and living the life of your dreams.

Chapter One

Realize Who You Are

No man can know where he is going unless he knows exactly where he has been and exactly how he has arrived at his present place.

— MAYA ANGELOU, POET, EDUCATOR, HISTORIAN

Why is having confidence in ourselves and our abilities so hard? Why do many of us have the tendency to overestimate other people's abilities and power and underestimate our own? Why are we so concerned with what other people will think about us?

If we are to understand these things, first we need to understand why we think, feel, and act the way we do. We need to understand why and how we have become who we are, as well as why we react or respond in certain ways. When we understand ourselves, we can either accept the way we are or make changes so we will be able to accept ourselves.

What we believe and accept about ourselves determines our behavior and performance. These, in turn, create our results and our results affect our confidence levels.

We behave in accordance with our beliefs about ourselves. If we have self-limiting beliefs, we will have self-limiting behaviors. If we have self-empowering beliefs, we will have self-empowering behaviors. In other words, if we think we can, we can and if we think we can't, we can't. If we think we can, we will find a way. We perform as well as we believe we are capable of performing.

Most of our beliefs about ourselves have come from outside sources: people, education, and experiences. Many of us have allowed the opinions of others to become our opinions of ourselves. We've listened to people tell us we are incompetent, inadequate, unworthy, bad, or stupid. We've internalized, processed, and often believed what others have told us.

There is a direct correlation between the quality of our relationships and our levels of self-esteem and self-confidence. If we are like most people, how we feel about ourselves, good or bad, is largely dependent upon the degree of acceptance we have felt from the influential people in our lives.

In the beginning, we learned our beliefs and values from our parents. If our parents' self-esteem levels were low or they had poor self-concepts, values, and beliefs, then that's what we learned. If they felt inferior, inadequate, or unworthy, we probably adopted those qualities. When we are children, we go through an "imprint period" where we formulate our behavior patterns based on what is impressed upon our thought patterns by the adults who are instrumental in our development.

If we were told "you are a bad girl," it really meant our behavior was unacceptable, but most of us didn't hear it that way. We internalized it to mean that **we** were unacceptable. Most parents don't realize how important it is to separate the act from the individual. Instead of saying, "You're usually so graceful; I'm surprised you tripped and fell. Are you okay?" they will say, "You're so clumsy!" They don't understand the deep, negative impact this has on a child.

If we were compared negatively to other children, especially children outside of our immediate family, we might have believed those children had more abilities and were more popular than we were. That is when feelings of inferiority start to set in. If we didn't receive appreciation or recognition for our achievements then, we may believe others are smarter, stronger, or better than we are now.

If my grandmother told me once, she told me a hundred times that my cousin, Bobbie, was smarter, cuter, and more popular than I was. After the first ten times, she really didn't have to tell me anymore. I already believed it! So if Bobbie took dance classes, I didn't want to take dance classes, because I knew before I started I would never be as good as she was. If Bobbie tried out for a part in the school play, I wouldn't try out, because I could never be as good as Bobbie. If Bobbie ran for student council, I certainly wouldn't be able to achieve what she achieved, so why bother? There was no point in being homecoming queen, because Bobbie had already worn that crown.

If we had parents who tried to realize their unfulfilled dreams through us and our accomplishments, they may have pushed us beyond our abilities or our desires in particular areas, making us feel "less than" we could have been or should have been. Or maybe they even instilled such a drive in us to be what they wanted us to be, that we didn't learn how to be assertive and stand up for what *we* wanted.

My friend, Sue, didn't want to play softball, but her father was the girls' softball coach and a jock to boot, so he insisted Sue become a pitcher and a home-run hitter. He pushed and pushed until she was in tears after every game and she quit before the end of the season! When she was in Girl Scouts and they went on a hike, Sue somehow wandered away from the others and became lost. Once found, her father said to her, "Don't tell anyone you couldn't find your way out of the woods." When they would go fishing, he would say to her before they ever got to the dock, "I know you are going to be sick, so just deal with it!" Today Sue works at a job she doesn't really enjoy, because she still hopes to win her father's approval and when she faces challenges in life, she sometimes cries, has a tendency to get sick, often quits things before learning to do them well and most of all, tries to "just deal with it." In other instances, she takes on risky assignments in an attempt to get her father to see how brave and strong she has become! Occasionally, I hear her reference how well she has done for a girl who can't find her way out of the woods. Is it as obvious to you as it is to me where these coping mechanisms were learned? Isn't it sad that her father's early harsh criticisms have stayed with her all of her life?

If our parents or peers were obsessed with physical appearance, they may have pushed us into a life that devalued us. Jeanette was a beautiful teenager. Her parents pushed her into every beauty contest they could find. They were determined, because she was so beautiful, she should have only the best of everything. They moved to the most exclusive neighborhood in the city, so she could go to the right school with a "higher class" of students. They joined the country club at great expense, so she could mingle with the "right" people; then they worked around the clock to pay for it. When she had the opportunity to meet young men, her mother would say, "Stand up and meet the boy." So Jeanette would stand up, stick out her breasts, suck in her stomach and put on her most seductive smile, so the boy could look her over and see what a good catch she would be. She married the man they chose for her who didn't appreciate her "standing up" to meet all his friends and business associates. She lived a miserable life and finally got divorced. Then she found herself back in the limelight standing up for the "right" men to meet her again. Unfortunately, as she grew older, her looks faded and she was no longer the beauty she had been. Because she relied completely on her beauty, she never developed any of the other interests, virtues, or qualities one might seek in a mate. She died bitter and alone — surrounded by her beauty pageant trophies.

Children of parents who are obsessed with physical appearance usually develop a major case of low self-esteem. In addition, the media puts so much emphasis on beauty and being thin that many girls, and even supposedly intelligent grown women, develop eating disorders and poor health in an effort to keep up their appearances.

If our parents placed a very high value on possessions and having money in the bank, whether they had it or not, the emphasis on materialism we learned could lead us to a life of overachievement and striving for wealth and material goods. We may even marry someone for his possessions, wealth, or stature.

Mary's occupation is marrying wealthy men. I say "men," because she has married four men of considerable means and found out after each wedding ceremony that she didn't even like them. Eventually each "wonderful" marriage ended up in a bitter, nasty divorce. How many of these do you think she'll go through before she realizes what she is doing? My father used to say, "If you marry someone, be sure you like the person and you can love him even if he loses everything he has, because that's the person you'll be stuck with." Times have changed since my father's day, and in today's world where two out of three marriages end in divorce, you no longer need to stay stuck in a bad relationship. You can get a divorce without the stigma it carried in my father's time, but why would you want to put yourself through all that turmoil and emotional drama? It's certainly hard on one's self-esteem. We shouldn't use up even one moment of our lives dealing with negative emotional feelings that we can avoid by making better choices in the first place.

If parents are unable to cope with tragedy, their child may feel as if whatever happened was her fault. A young woman of a family I was counseling revealed to me she had been raped several years before, but had not had any previous therapy. Upon inquiry, her father said, "Well, it was her own fault. She runs around with the wrong people and was in the wrong place at the wrong time." Rape is not the victim's fault! It is a crime of violence and it is a horrible experience. The victim must get counseling. She must be helped to understand that she is a person with great personal worth and given as much support as possible to help regain her self-esteem and self-confidence.

Parents very often cripple their children emotionally and cause their children to feel inadequate, not because they mean to, but because they are overly permissive or overly possessive. In many cases, these children never learn self-discipline, self-reliance or responsibility. These are the very characteristics that help us achieve. Achievement builds self-esteem.

When I was modeling, there was another model I worked with whose daughter was an absolute terror. Whenever this model would bring her daughter into the agency or backstage at a fashion show, the child would create havoc. The kid was into everything. She ran through the building screaming and would often hang on the racks which were full of clothing for the shows. Occasionally, this child would even pull designer gowns off the rack and onto the floor. Her mother would tell her to stop, sit down and behave, but of course, she never did and it was never reinforced. As a teenager, her mother let her run wild. She went where she wanted with whomever she wanted. She had no curfew and was seldom disciplined. She became pregnant, quit school, and moved in with her boyfriend. A year later she was arrested, along with the boyfriend, for drug dealing and sentenced to two years in prison. Her mother accepted no responsibility. She told everyone she could never do anything with the girl, because her daughter had inherited her father's genes.

Accepting hand-me-down feelings

Am I saying we can inherit our self-esteem or lack of it? No. Not through the genes anyway. What I'm saying is if we are not aware and don't consciously do something about it, we can pass our level of self-esteem from one generation to the next. That's okay if we have high self-esteem, but if we have low self-esteem, it's often disastrous.

Low self-esteem brings with it some behavioral problems which are exhibited in our everyday lives. It is important we recognize whether or not we demonstrate any of these behaviors.

Negativity seeking

People with low self-esteem often find fault with others. If we don't like ourselves, we tend not to like other people, either. We may think if we can find something wrong with others, it will make us better. We are actually attempting to make ourselves feel better at their expense. Coincidentally, the traits we don't like in other people are usually the very same traits we don't like in ourselves. If you are a fault-finder, here's a homework assignment for you. Try to get through the next 24 hours without expressing one negative comment about anyone or anything. You need to break the habit of seeking negativity. When you see something you don't like about someone, immediately make yourself look for something good about that same person. The more you look for good, the more you will find.

Hungry for attention

Most people enjoy other people showing an interest in them. People with low self-esteem and a lack of confidence sometimes make every effort to be the center of attention. They talk incessantly about themselves, their accomplishments, what they own, who they know, and where they have been. There is no exchange of information. It is all about "me, myself, and I." If they do ask a question, they usually want to know what you think about them. This is really just a cry for acceptance. They are impressed with you and want your approval. They want you to believe they are someone worth knowing. Unfortunately, their behavior usually has the opposite effect.

If you find you are one of these people, instead of trying to get all the attention, make an effort to make other people feel special. In this day and age, people are so caught up in themselves they don't put any effort into making others feel important.

Stop and think. When was the last time someone really made you feel special? What can you do to show other people you are glad they are in your world?

The biggest psychological need most people have is to be understood. Why not start by listening to others? Ask them questions about themselves and about their lives, and then listen attentively. Show interest in what they have to say. Lean forward. Comment on what they have said before you start telling your own story. Compliment them on things they do well.

The more you make other people feel special, the more attention you will receive and that will build your confidence.

In Jesse Ferrell's book, *How You Leave Them Feeling*, he shares a story of a call he received from a college buddy he had not seen in over six years. After talking about their lives and how glad they were to talk again, the college buddy said he needed to ask Jesse a favor. It seems the buddy's mother was dying of cancer and when he asked his mother if she had any last wishes, she said, "If I could see Jesse Ferrell just one more time before I die, that would be great. Jesse's positive attitude helped me so much whenever I was around him during your college days and my transition to this big city. That would truly make me happy."

Jesse must feel wonderful knowing he made such a positive impact on someone's life that even after more than six years, her last request was to see him one more time. Would that give you confidence? Would that let you know your life had purpose? It certainly would me.

Choosing to be a loner

Loners usually don't like to be around other people because they lack the confidence to handle themselves in social situations. They are more comfortable being alone, because it is easier than expending the energy to have a pleasing personality or show interest in other people. In many cases, they don't know how to be a friend. They really don't care about anyone else. When they do get around people, they are often aggressive, critical, or have an obsessive need to be right.

People who have a need to be "right" are in some way trying to convince themselves they are as good as or better than the next person. This is simply a lack of self-esteem.

My neighbor's husband died nine years ago. Before his death, they had eyes only for each other and didn't socialize much. After his death, she became reclusive. I kept inviting her for lunch or dinner and, eventually, she would accept. As the years went by, she came to dinner when someone insisted, but she always dominated the conversation, interrupted and corrected other guests, and often talked loudly over other people's conversations. Her contributions to the conversations were about herself and her illnesses, aches, and pains. She didn't read a newspaper, watch television, or listen to the radio, so if anyone attempted to talk about current events, she would change the conversation back to her past. Then the next day, she would call me to criticize everything, including how much she disliked most of the other people I invited. The neighbor who lived on the other side of her also invited her to dinner or to go shopping and to lunch. This woman would occasionally go, never offer to pay, and then would call me to complain about the woman who invited her.

She often mentioned how much she liked to be alone and how she deliberately didn't answer the phone or return calls, because she didn't want to talk to people. She never invited anyone to do anything with her or to visit her home. She didn't volunteer or participate in any groups. Her actions pushed people away. When we tried to find out what she might be interested in, she would tell us she had no desire to do anything but "sit on the sofa and think."

Feeling depressed

Let's face it, life is not always easy, and for some people, depression very often takes over. We get depressed when we are discouraged or disappointed in ourselves or our lives. We start to feel as though we can't live up to the expectations of others . . . or even our own expectations. We feel inadequate to handle what needs to be handled, to do what needs to be done, or to be what we think we should be. The attempt to live up to these expectations can be both a cause of low self-esteem and an effect of low self-esteem. It can even lead to overindulgence in food, alcohol, tobacco, drugs, or sex in an attempt to satisfy some need we have to make ourselves feel better in some way, or to dull the pain we are feeling. Ironically, this overindulgence simply adds to our feelings of worthlessness. We criticize ourselves for being weak and indulging in unhealthy practices. This self-criticism feeds the depression even more. It's a vicious cycle.

People who are depressed sometimes try to escape ... from themselves and from the world. I knew a young woman some years ago who used sleeping pills to "escape" from the difficulties she was having. Her situation became worse because she couldn't or wouldn't face her realities. Eventually, she had to be hospitalized. At one point, she wouldn't even comb her hair. Because she got professional help, today she is a fully functioning executive with a happy personal relationship and two well-adjusted adult children.

If you are caught up in depression, get some therapy right away. Severe depression can develop into self-hate, self-rejection, and a desire to end your own life, possibly even the reality of acting on that desire. This is not how you should live. Your life experience should be a wonderful journey, full of joy and excitement. Get professional help now, so you can get back to yourself, the self you know you can be ... a person with a purpose and passion for living.

Need to control

When one person has a compulsive need to control, dominate, possess, or run another person's life, it is usually because of an incredible need to be loved. This person's extremely low self-esteem causes her to feel inadequate and insecure. In an attempt not to let anyone know how she really feels, she becomes greedy and self-centered. She is not really interested in the welfare of others. She is attempting to fill her own need for self-worth. Unfortunately, it is usually done at the expense of others.

Jane knows something about everything. No matter what you want to do or where you want to go, she tells you of something or some place better. She tells you how to run your family, your career, your organization, and your business. She tells you where you should eat dinner and which restaurants have gotten too many demerits by the health department, so you shouldn't eat in any of those. She insists on driving, and whenever you are going anywhere together, she picks you up in her car because she must be able to leave when she is ready. Conversation is always about her – her life, her successes, or how much better she could have done what you just did. She chooses the outing, provides the tickets, and then calls to tell you she's already done it for you, without checking to see if you would like to go or not. If you say you can't go, she begs and pleads, becomes angry, accuses you of being ungrateful, and makes it your fault. Because she has no personal self-confidence, she has to show herself and everyone else she is in control. She's not a happy person. She's not happy with her life. She's not happy with her relationships, which never last very long anyway. Most of all, she's not happy with herself.

Trying to be perfect

Another type of control freak is the perfectionist. She is trying to control her own life to make sure she, and everything she does, is always perfect. She must have the perfect house, the perfect car, the perfect kids, the perfect husband, the perfect friends, the perfect personal grooming, and the perfect outfit. Absolutely everything must be perfect. This puts a lot of pressure on everyone around her, as well as on herself. The quest for perfection is a nightmare. It can lead to extreme stress and to procrastination. If she can't do it perfectly, then she'll just put it off, believing she will have the time to do it perfectly later on, although that time never comes. In the meantime, a lot of tasks remain undone. She starts to feel bad about them not getting done, becomes more stressed, and her self-esteem suffers. She doesn't have the confidence to go forward, because she's not perfect. If this describes you in any way, you need to realize that perfection is an implausible goal. Given the speed at which our lives are being lived, it is impossible to do everything perfectly. Give yourself a break and get over this need for perfection. Excellence is good enough.

Wallowing in self-pity

Low self-esteem sometimes manifests itself as "pity parties." This type of person thinks, "I can't seem to get control over my life so, therefore, I am at the mercy of people, circumstances, and conditions that keep me from doing, being, and having what I really want." These people look for something or someone to blame so they don't have to take charge or do something about their situation! My mom used to tell me that, "People can't let you down unless you are leaning on them." It is up to you to be a confident person. No one else can hurt your feelings, upset you, or make you angry. It is your choice whether or not you become affected by what other people say or do. What you think about what they say or do dictates your reaction. If you want to be a confident person, then change your thoughts. You, and only you, are responsible for your thoughts, your feelings, and your life.

When I was visiting one of my friends recently, her sister was also visiting. Her sister was there to seek comfort, because her husband had left her for her best friend. She dwelled on this day and night and talked of nothing else. I felt very sorry for her and tried to console her. She spoke about how she was determined to get him back. It wasn't until the end of my trip, two weeks later, that I learned it had been seven years since her husband left her. In fact, he had married the other woman six years ago. Her chances of getting him back were slim and none. My friend's sister was stuck in her pity party and wouldn't move on with her life. It got in the way of her joy, her success, and her ability to establish new relationships. Why is she stuck? Why does she choose to live in the past? She is more comfortable in her familiar discomfort than she would be in a new, unfamiliar world of dating and meeting someone new. She knows how to wallow in her grief and self-pity, so she does. Unfortunately, her repetitive, sad story became tiresome and boring to others.

Expressing criticism

Whenever I hear someone say, "Would you like a little constructive criticism?" I cringe. I don't believe there is any such thing as constructive criticism! All criticism is destructive.

When we criticize another person, it undermines that person. No one wants to hear someone say, "Let me tell you what's wrong with you." That's what criticism does. Telling someone what's wrong with her can add to any feelings of inadequacy or incompetence she may already have. She may get her feelings hurt, get angry, or have a need to retaliate. None of this is helpful.

When a child gets criticized, it causes self-doubt, creates poor self-image and can even break her spirit, causing her to give up on her dreams, ambitions, and desires. In addition, it teaches her to criticize herself, creating feelings of inferiority — feeling she is not "good enough" and she learns to run herself down. When someone offers her a genuine compliment or accolade, she has trouble believing it to be true. Criticism undermines self-esteem and decreases effectiveness.

The mother of one of my friends has a tendency to be overly direct and not at all tactful. Whenever the mother is confronted by her criticism of others, she says, "Well, it's better to tell them the truth and let them deal with it." As a consequence of her mother's outspoken criticism, my friend often has the feeling she is "less than." When I asked her what "less than" meant to her, she said, "Not good enough. Less than my mother expects. Less than my sister is. Less than I probably could be." I know her mother is proud of her. I don't believe this mother ever intended to make her daughter feel insecure, but that's what criticism does . . . especially if it is constant.

If your desire is truly to help someone become better, to have more, or to improve her performance, then say, "Would you like an idea of how you might do that easier? Or quicker? Or better?" Or, "May I suggest how you could improve your performance?" Most of us welcome suggestions and ideas. These are conducive to building self-esteem and confidence.

If someone offers you some constructive criticism, why not smile and say in a warm tone of voice, "I would welcome any suggestions you have for how I could improve. I would appreciate you keeping any criticism to a minimum."

Making conscious choices

We can improve our confidence by modifying our destructive behaviors. We can accomplish this by making conscious choices to think about ourselves in a more positive manner. We must reprogram the subconscious portion of our minds. This part of our minds has no judging function; it only processes information. It follows our instructions. It is up to us to instruct it properly in order to create the self-image and self-confidence we wish to have.

One of the most effective ways to help your subconscious see things differently is the use of affirmations. An affirmation is a statement you make to yourself to affirm something is true, even in the face of all evidence to the contrary. Human thought can only affirm, for even when it denies, it is affirming that denial to be true.

Repeating an affirmation leads the mind to a state of consciousness that accepts what you wish it to believe. If you wish to be confident, then use the affirmation, "I am a confident person." Don't say, "I am nervous or afraid," because you would be affirming the opposite of what you truly desire, which is to be confident. Write out your affirmation and put it where you will see it over and over throughout the day. Look at it, read it, think about it, and what it can mean to your life. Do this every day to ensure positive changes taking place in your consciousness, attitude, and environment.

Don't expect this to be easy. Your subconscious has had years of programming to get it to perform the way it does at this time. You aren't going to undo all of that overnight. If you want to be confident and successful and you are willing to do the work, it will happen!

Stop criticizing yourself

Stop talking about your negative traits. The more you concentrate on them, the more they hang on. What we put our attention to is what multiplies in our lives. Instead of criticizing, look for things you like about yourself.

If you have actual limitations you can't do anything about, then you need to accept them. The things most of us complain about are the things we *can* do something about.

If you feel you are too short or too tall, there is nothing you can do about that. You might as well learn to look at the advantages of being short or tall. I saw Michael J. Fox interviewed on television early in his career. The interviewer asked Michael how he felt about being so short, just 5 feet, 4 inches. Michael became animated and shared how he has always seen his size as an advantage! Most of us know someone with a "Napoleonic Complex" or feelings of inadequacy directly related to being short. Those people usually try to compensate by driving big cars, having big desks, or acting just plain nasty. Instead, Michael J. Fox was proud of his height and shared how much he enjoys being smaller. He said when he was younger, his family got locked out of the house and he was the one who could squeeze through the basement window to let everyone in. He has embraced a characteristic over which he has no control.

If you feel you are too heavy or too thin, you can do something about that. If you don't like the color of your skin or the texture of your hair, that's too bad. You'd be smart to realize the advantages you have being the way you are. If you don't like the shape of your eyebrows, the color of your hair, or even the size of your breasts, in this day and age, there's no reason not to change those into what you want. If your body isn't shaped the way you want it, change your diet or go to the gym. If you don't make enough money to have a gym membership, walk around the block, go to the YWCA, or better still, find a better paying job, so you can afford to go to the gym and have the other things you desire as well. You could move into an apartment or condominium complex that has a gym, get a job with a company that has a gym, or go online to find out all of the ways you can exercise that don't cost a dime. Concentrate on what you *can* do, not what you can't.

If there is something you can change to make you feel better about yourself, then for goodness sake, change it. Don't whine about it.

People don't want to be around someone who whines and complains all the time. Most of the things we complain about are things other people wouldn't have even noticed until we brought them to their attention. How can you be self-confident when you keep focusing on what's wrong with you? The image you have of yourself influences all of your experiences.

False images of ourselves

Somewhere along the line you may have come to believe you are not good enough to be the person you want to be or have the things you want. Somehow your attitudes, feelings, possessions, and what you do have gotten all mixed up with who you are. You may *feel* if you don't *do* something exceptionally well, you can't *be* someone exceptionally good. When you feel you are competent or above average at what you do, this reinforces the feeling you are someone of value. The more you accomplish, the better you feel about yourself.

At the same time, the quality of our relationships can affect our self-confidence. Many of us base our self-esteem on whether or not we are accepted and loved by other people. Do they find me physically attractive? Do they think I am smart? Do they like my personality? Do they think I'm funny? Do they want to be with me?

Before you can expect anyone else to accept you, you must first accept yourself. The more you like yourself, the more confident you will be. That will give you a more positive outlook and a more positive attitude. In turn, you'll be healthier and happier. When you are healthy and happy, you are more attractive to other people. They find you to be smart, clever, and humorous and want to be with you.

You can't give to anyone else that which you don't have to give. Everything you do to raise your own level of self-love will improve the quality of all of your relationships. It's time to start accepting yourself.

Your behavior is consistent with your thoughts

You are who you are right now because of your past thoughts about yourself. You can deliberately become who you want to be by changing your thoughts. We change our thoughts by changing our mental pictures. Put a picture in your mind of you at your best. Clearly visualize how you would stand, walk, talk, dress, and behave if you could be who and what you really want to be. Visualize yourself as someone people notice, want to get to know, want to please, and with whom they want to enjoy either a personal or professional relationship. Hold that picture in your mind and start to act "as if" you already are that person. Stand the way that person would stand. Walk and talk the way that person would walk and talk. Dress and behave in the same manner as the ideal picture in your mind. See yourself as having the attributes and qualities of your ideal self. Live them as if you have them! Quit being and seeing whatever you think you are now and start being and seeing only what you want to be. And guess what? By assuming the role you wish to become, one day you'll realize you really are that person.

Confidence comes when we determine that we are responsible for ourselves; when we are able to stand on our own two feet, make our own decisions, and deal with the consequences of our own behaviors and choices. Don't listen to anyone who tries to make you believe someone else is superior, more intelligent, or able to make better decisions than you. If you make your own decisions, you will deal with the consequences of your decisions. If you let others make your decisions, you still have to deal with the consequences of the decisions, but they will be based on someone else's choices . . . not yours.

Free advice is usually worth what you paid for it

There are a lot of people willing to give you "some free advice." They want to tell you what you could do, should do, or what they would do if they were you. But they aren't you! They don't feel your feelings. They can't solve your problems or live your life. Only you can do that. Whenever you have a decision to make, research the situation and your options. Get all the information you can from reliable sources before you make a decision. Then make sure the ultimate decision is yours.

Listen to your inner voice

Your inner voice usually knows what's best. If you will take the time to realistically look at each problem, challenge, or situation and ask yourself, "What one thing can I do now to make this better or to move in the direction of a solution?" you will soon meet your life's challenges with self-assurance and confidence.

There is a direct correlation between our achievement in life and the confidence we have in ourselves. We perform as well as we believe we will. Whenever we feel good about ourselves and are doing well . . . whether in our relationships or our careers . . . we are demonstrating our self-confidence. Whenever we allow the opinions of others to influence our opinion of ourselves, we give others power over us and we base our self-image on false ideas and concepts. Many of us are still allowing the opinions others had of us years ago to affect our reality today. Give them up. The clearer you are about who you are and the person you want to become, the more you will be able to do the things you want to do and have the things you want to have.

You know in your heart you can either accept things as they are or take the responsibility to change them. You will be happier if you feel you have control over your own circumstances. Don't be a victim who sits around stuck in fear and bad habits, just waiting for your luck to change, believing you are always in the wrong place at the wrong time or even thinking you must wait for the planets to align.

Be yourself

Work to be an independent person who does important things. When we are constantly trying to be what others want us to be and do what they want us to do, we lose ourselves. Instead, choose to step out of your comfort zone. Set a goal and make a plan to do something different or bigger. Take a risk and take action toward that goal.

We must develop our inner strength in order to express our individuality. Set high personal standards for yourself and for your work. Put more time and effort into what you do. Be the best at what you do.

My business partner and I had a consulting job for a riverboat casino. One night, as we were walking through the casino observing the customer service, we noticed one of the blackjack tables had approximately ten customers lined up waiting behind every chair. These customers were waiting for a turn to play at this particular table while other tables had chairs that were empty. We pushed our way up to where we could see the dealer. The dealer, Buster, was phenomenal. He was very professional dealing the cards, and at the same time, he was extremely entertaining and funny. He was different than the others. He was unique. He seemed to love his job. Certainly, if I was going to play blackjack, I'd want to be at Buster's table rather than at the table of another dealer who had no personality. Night after night, we walked through the casino to check the service and every night was the same. People would wait to play at Buster's table rather than play at a table with a dealer who was not fun and entertaining. You'd think the other dealers would figure it out, wouldn't you?

Find ways to express your uniqueness

When you are able to express your uniqueness, you will feel more complete. Learn to accept yourself for who you are and focus on what you want to become. There's no one else exactly like you. You are one very special individual who was created to be who you are — doing the best you can each day to get the best results life has to offer. Learn to love yourself with all your strengths and all your weaknesses. Remember, weaknesses provide you with opportunities for growth. Respect yourself. Your primary responsibility is your own physical and emotional well-being. When you are true to yourself and learn to take care of you, your self-respect will grow.

We have so much more to offer the world than just a shadow of ourselves. Give up old hurts and old scars. Give up negative thinking. Keep forgiving yourself for any mistakes you have made. Congratulate yourself for taking risks. Give up your negative self-image. It will keep you from achieving the success you want and deserve.

Many of us undermine our confidence by trying to earn the approval of others. For some reason, we seem to think if we can get the approval of those around us, things will be better or others will take care of us. The truth is, no one but you is going to take care of you. You need to become very clear about that. No matter how much someone else loves you or you love that person, you still need to take care of yourself.

Until you learn how to rely on yourself, you will have to depend on your ability to influence others to fulfill your needs. That will leave you at the mercy of those upon whom you depend. You will never be able to have or do more than you can convince them to allow you to have or do.

You owe it to yourself to learn to depend on yourself to meet your own wants, needs, and expectations. This doesn't mean you have to be alone. It means you need to know that, if and when you are alone, you are still more than enough. You know who you are and what your values are. You let your values guide your life and your decisions. You aren't going through this life just to be a people pleaser. Overcoming dependency isn't easy. That's why so many people are stuck in co-dependent relationships. When you are confident, you can be yourself whether alone, with someone else, or in a group of people.

There are things you can do to make the transition to independence less difficult.

Stop demanding perfection from yourself

When you do your best, your best is good enough. Realize that in order to do something well, we usually have to do it poorly at first. Liberace had to learn to play the piano. He certainly didn't play it on his first day as well as he did when he was a performer on the Las Vegas strip. Venus and Serena Williams weren't professional tennis players the day they started. They first had to learn how to hit the ball. You can't expect to do something with perfection the first time you try. The key is to keep trying until you become proficient. And even then, you will still want to practice and improve. Although Michelle Wie is a professional golfer, she is still perfecting her skills every day. When my friend, Charlotte, was learning to dance, she fell down many times, making her very frustrated and discouraged. Her dance instructor told her, "Don't worry about it. You must fall one hundred times before you are a dancer." So she picked herself up, kept trying and practicing. It wasn't long before she was a dancer who worked professionally in Las Vegas production shows. How many falls would it have taken before you gave up? When we don't do something well at first, many of us quit, instead of keeping on until we are proficient at doing it. When we don't get recognition from others or rewards for making the attempt, but get criticism instead, we may be embarrassed and think we look stupid or even worse, that we are stupid, which is our excuse for giving up.

Rewards don't have to come from others

Reward yourself when you've made an effort toward learning something new or doing something you've never done before. Reward yourself even if you didn't do it very well. Reward yourself for having the guts to get out there and try. Taking the action was the important part.

My dad was a salesman. One day, when I was a teenager, he dropped his appointment notebook on the floor. When it fell open, I noticed there were gold stars on many of the pages. I asked him why a grown man would have gold stars pasted in his book. He told me he gave himself a gold star every day just for getting through the day. On the days when he made a sale, he put lots of gold stars on the page. He said it kept him focused on what went right in his life. On the days things weren't going so well, he'd flip back through the pages and look at his gold stars. They would remind him of what was going right in his life and career. In spite of what was happening that day, he could see he was successful. What my Dad was doing back then, though he didn't have a name for it, was "anchoring" his self-esteem.

When you anchor something, you are holding it in place. Just as a ship's anchor keeps it from drifting with the ever-present currents and tides, personal anchoring keeps you from drifting off your course.

Every time my dad stuck a gold star on a page, he was telling himself, "I'm okay."

I was sixteen when I got my first job and started the practice of giving myself stars, just like my dad. I've been doing it ever since. Today there are lots of motivational stickers that you can buy. They say things like "Way to Go," "You're # 1," "Nice Job," "Awesome," "Excellent," "Hooray," and "You're a Superstar." So buy some stickers for yourself and when you achieve one of your goals, when you take positive action, or even when you just get through a rough day, put a sticker in your daily diary or your goal achievement journal. You'll be anchoring your own self-esteem.

One of my former employees gave me a pair of gold star earrings as a thank-you gift when she left my employ, along with a card that said, "You were the best boss I ever had." I wear those earrings almost every day. When I look in the mirror, it anchors my self-esteem. It tells me I was a great employer and the "best boss" she ever had.

The Christmas before my life partner passed away, he gave me a necklace with a gold star. On the back of it was engraved, "Until the 12th of Never." The card read, "You are the best partner a man could ever have." I wear the necklace often to remind myself I was a good partner and he was happier while I was in his life than he had ever been before. The engraved message was his way of telling me he would love me forever.

Reminding ourselves of our achievements, our worth, and our value to others is imperative. Physical reminders help you to concentrate on the positive things in your life and recognize that any feelings of inadequacy you may have are carry-overs from your past. Most feelings of insecurity we have were acquired through someone else's negative perceptions and influence.

Be sure not to let the opinions of others become more important to you than your own opinion of you. Get yourself some gold stars or some motivational stickers and reward yourself regularly.

You *can* achieve self-confidence. It's a choice. You can free yourself from dependency, conformity, comparison, manipulation, and competition. You **can** do the things that make your heart sing. You **can** learn to depend on yourself for your own success and your own happiness. You are one of a kind — uniquely yourself — unlike anyone else. There are no two things in this universe exactly alike. No two trees, no two clouds, no two snowflakes, no two blades of grass, no two grains of sand are exactly alike, and there's no two of you even if you're an identical twin. You are the only "you" there is. Realize who you are, because you are more than enough.

Realization Exercise

Before you can choose a new direction in life, you need to know who you are and what strengths you have. Imagine you have just run into a friend you haven't seen in a long time and you are telling this person every good thing you can think of about yourself and every accomplishment you have achieved. List them below.

1. _____

_____

_____

_____

2. _____

_____

_____

_____

3. _____

_____

_____

_____

4. _____

_____

_____

_____

5. _____

_____

_____

_____

6. _____

_____

_____

_____

7. _____

_____

_____

_____

Realization Affirmation

I am more than enough. There is no one who can be a better me than I can. I am complete just as I am. My mind, my heart and my skills expand to meet each new challenge and need with ease. There is always enough of me to share — with plenty to spare. I am complete. I am more than enough.

Chapter Two

Explore Your Possibilities

Without leaps of imagination, or dreaming, we lose the excitement of possibilities. Dreaming, after all, is a form of planning.

— **GLORIA STEINEM**
FEMINIST LEADER, AUTHOR

On New Year's Eve, many people write down their resolutions for the year ahead and before the year is half over, they have usually forgotten all about them. The next year, they list the same things they didn't achieve the year before. I believe they do this because they haven't attached their goals to a purpose.

Many of us make resolutions pertaining to our weight. Year after year we write the goal for our weight loss or weight gain. Then the 20-year high school reunion comes up and that's the year we lose or gain the desired weight. We achieve our goal because we have a purpose. We want everyone to say we still look as good as we did back then. Or we want a man to see what a mistake he made choosing another girl over us. I wanted Richard Willert to regret paying Bill Pulliam $10.00 to take me off his hands at the homecoming dance during my junior year in high school. Now that's a purpose!

People who give up half-way through the year usually haven't decided where they really want to go or looked at all the possible ways to get there. All they did was make a wish list. These are the same people that we hear later on in life saying, "I wish I had done this," or "I regret I didn't do that."

You want to live your life so you never look back with regrets. Take steps to reach your goals in the fastest and best manner possible. What steps can you take right now toward finding what you love and doing it? Which path will you take? How will you know that path is the best choice?

Brainstorm

This is a technique we use to examine all of the possibilities and potential solutions, without making judgments about any of these possibilities until we have exhausted all of our options.

Dr. Alex Osborn, the originator of the *Brainstorming Technique,* and co-founder of what was one of the world's largest advertising agencies in the 1960's, Batten, Barton, Durstine & Osborne, as well as the founder of the Creative Education Foundation, described this method of thinking as "organized ideation." He believed that, "When you drive for new ideas, you shouldn't drive with your brakes on."

His method proved to be so effective that many top companies and organizations around the world still use it today. If it's good enough for them, I certainly believe it's good enough for you or me. Whether you choose to use this technique by yourself or with other people, there are some rules to follow.

Quantity of ideas is more important than quality

Write down ideas, lots of ideas, about what you think you would or could love to do, have, or be in your life. The more ideas we have, the better our chances are of finding what we want.

No idea is too outrageous

All ideas are welcome. The more ideas you have, the better your chance of finding what you want. Right now, you are looking for possibilities. If you think you might like to be an astronaut, write that down. Would you like to live in a castle in Germany? Write it down. Would you like to go back to school? Find the perfect partner? It doesn't matter what you put down, as long as you think you might really love to do it, become it, or have it. It's okay to be a bit "out there" in your wants and dreams. You might list things like:

- ★ Take belly-dancing lessons

- ★ Explore Denali National Park and Preserve in Alaska

- ★ Go on an elephant-back safari through the Okavango Swamp

- ★ Dive the Great Barrier Reef

- ★ Start your own business

- ★ Marry the boss

- ★ Climb Mount Fuji

- ★ Work overseas for a year to gain international experience

- ★ Hang out in a coffee shop in the shadow of the Eiffel Tower

The following day, get the list out and add to it. Do this for several days. You will be amazed at the number of possibilities you will come up with.

When you have all the options you can possibly think of, ask yourself some creativity questions and write your answers on a separate piece of paper. Apply these questions to every possibility you have listed.

Some questions you might ask are:

- ★ What activities or goals can I combine to get a better outcome?

- ★ How can I rearrange my schedule? Or my finances?

- ★ Can I do more of something? Less of something?

- ★ What can I adapt, modify, or do differently?

- ★ What if I gave up something or added something?

- ★ Can I do the opposite of what I've been doing?

Again, remember not to make judgments. Just write down your ideas. Many of your ideas will be wild and crazy and maybe even things you can't use. That's okay. Somewhere in there will be a great idea you **can** use.

Criticism is NOT allowed

Criticism is negative and kills ideas. Creating the idea and evaluating the idea are two different things. At this stage, you are simply creating ideas. Don't say anything negative to yourself or to others when you are using this technique. Immediately stop anyone who begins to evaluate, is negative, or critical. Explain you are not in the evaluation phase yet.

Evaluate and improve

Once you have a lot of ideas, look them over, think about them, and ask yourself, "Is this workable? Practical? Financially feasible?" If your answers are "No," then ask, "Could it be made to be workable or practical? Is there a less expensive way to do it?" Eliminate any options you are absolutely positive won't work.

After you've decided which ideas you are going to keep, rewrite them on a separate sheet of paper. Put the new list away and think about your ideas for a couple of days.

When you take out the paper again, write the positives and negatives of each idea listed. Some of your ideas will have so many negatives, they will practically eliminate themselves.

What you'll have left are a couple of good ideas which have been thoroughly evaluated. You can now make a safe, sound decision as to which of these ideas to use or how to combine them to get the results you want.

If you use this technique, you will find more possibilities than you imagined and your ultimate decision will be much more exciting and effective than if you had just gone with your first option.

The secret to getting what you love

The secret to getting what you love is to believe it's possible. But how do you believe it's possible if you are unsure?

First, find out everything you can about what it is you want to try. Do your research. Find out what parts might be easy, what might be hard, what might be good, and what might be bad. The more you find out, the more uncertainty you eliminate. This will help to alleviate your fears.

If you are still unsure, sit down and figure out what it is about your ideas and goals that makes you hesitate. Do you feel like you just don't have the education or the skills necessary? Do you feel you lack the interpersonal skills to get along with people? Maybe you feel you don't have the work experience, the time, the money, the energy, or the resources.

Give up the Fear

Let's face it, the only thing that's really holding you back is fear . . . the Fear of Failure. Believe me; we **all** suffer from it at one time or another. We all have thoughts like, "Oh, I couldn't do that. I might fail and then where would I be? Look what I will have given up to try something new and if I fail, I'll have nothing. I won't be able to support my family, myself, or pay my bills. And besides, what will people think?" Sound familiar? Let me assure you, **you have nothing to fear**! You can **be**, **do**, and **have** anything in life that you want. What do you dream about? A great relationship? A bigger house in a better neighborhood? A luxurious vacation each year? A job that's fulfilling? A new car? It's all within your reach, no matter what your situation is now.

Thinking about staying behind?

When we have a fear of failure, we are putting our energy into failing. We become what we think about — so if fear of failure is always on our minds, what are we most likely to attract into our lives? You guessed it — **failure**! We are concentrating on failure and therefore, directing our subconscious mind to make us fail. When we think about our failures on a daily basis, we are simply rehearsing our upcoming results. Do you often find yourself thinking, "I can't do it because I'm not smart enough, attractive enough, educated enough, or thin enough?" Do you concentrate on the things you don't have or can't do such as, "I don't read music, speak another language, drive a car, or know how to golf?" Negative. Negative. Negative. "I can't." "I'm not." "I don't." You've rehearsed this stuff long enough. You might as well go ahead and finish the whine. "Everybody hates me. Nobody likes me. I'm gonna eat some worms and die." At some point you have to stop worrying about what people think and just get on with it. Accept the responsibility for your own success and be determined to move forward from this point!

When I was a young woman, my mom pointed out to me there is nothing wrong with failure. You sometimes have to fail in order to succeed. Here is the example she gave me: "When you were a child, you learned by trial and error. When you were learning to walk, it was not a game. Neither was it a test you could pass or fail. It was skill- building. You were learning a skill that you would need throughout your lifetime. If you fell down, no one said, 'That's it. You had one chance and you messed up. You get no more chances. Stay down.' No, when you fell down, we encouraged you to get up and try again. Then one day, you did it all by yourself. That's how it works. You try. You fall down. You get back up. You fall again. You get back up again and again until you get the result you want."

There's nothing written in the rule book of life that says you get one try and only one. Persistence is, in fact, one of the attributes of most successful people. Persistence means to go on resolutely in spite of opposition. It also means to go back and be willing to change things. You must decide what you want and then go after it. You can modify the process until you get the result you want. If you keep doing the same old thing in the same old way, you'll keep getting the same old result. If you want a new result, you must do something differently.

What will other people think?

Most of us have been taught we should be concerned about what others think about us and we should seek their approval for all we do. We hear a little voice in our heads yelling, "If you fail, you'll look like a fool."

When I was in high school, I didn't try out to be a cheerleader because I was afraid I wouldn't be as good as the other girls and wouldn't get selected for the squad. There it was --my fear of failure. In my mind, if I was rejected, it would mean I failed. So I decided it would be better not to try at all than to try, fail, and look like a fool. The sad part is that with my energy and enthusiasm, I'd have made a great cheerleader. Would my life have been different if I had been a cheerleader? I will never know, because I was too afraid to try. I'll bet you can look at your life and remember times when you were too afraid to try. We've all wondered about how our lives might be different now if we had taken a few more chances, instead of succumbing to the fear of failure.

What's wrong with failure anyway? Why do we let it stop us from doing, achieving, and having what we want? Failure just means you've discovered one more way that doesn't work. Thomas Edison worked for more than a year and a half to create a better, long-lasting light bulb that could be used in a mainstream application. During that time he found 9,999 ways that didn't work. If he hadn't persisted, you might be reading this book by candlelight! If you try and still don't get the result you want, it simply means you were willing to risk, it might take longer than you expected, your goal was unreasonable, you have to do something differently next time, or you have an opportunity to start something new which is more suited to you.

Wouldn't it be wonderful if we could just overcome this fear? We know there's always a chance we will fail, so why worry about it? Everyone else has the same chance of failure as we do. We are not the exception to the rule, but we will never succeed unless we try.

Life is an experiment

In life, you try one thing, it works. You try another, it doesn't work. Instead of letting it paralyze you, do some self-analysis. What went right? What went wrong? What went right that could have gone wrong? What other possibilities are there? Then do something differently. Be deliberate and take reasonable risks. Break down the process into smaller more manageable steps. Put the proper effort into achieving your goals and go after what you want. Keep on trying until you get the desired result.

When you have a goal, a dream, or you see an opportunity but you need help to get what you want, let someone know. People will help you if you ask them. If they don't know you want something, they will give it to someone else. Be clear. Don't just drop hints. Other people can't read your mind. They don't know what you dream about or what you'd like to become. Ask for help and accept it when offered.

Or are you just going to give up?

Giving up — even once — makes it easier and more acceptable to decide to "just give up" again. When you give up, you damage your self-respect. Your heart doesn't listen to the excuses for quitting which are created by your mind. Your heart knows that when you quit — when you give up — a little piece of your self-esteem dies each time until nothing is left. When you want something and go after it, even if you don't get it, you will at least know you made the effort and knowing you've done something will boost your self-respect. The biggest regret people ever have when they look back over their life experiences is they didn't go after something they wanted to have, do, or be. You don't want to wake up one day and discover you could have had something, achieved a goal, or done something significant, but didn't even try because you were too afraid to attempt it or believed you would fail. If you make the effort, you may just surprise yourself with what you are able to do.

One day when my father was trying to encourage my brother to finish a project, I heard him say, "You're very smart. You can solve this. Don't give up."

Then my brother said, "But I just can't get it!"

Daddy responded to my brother with one of his familiar lectures. "Son, the people we remember are those who didn't give up . . . Abraham Lincoln faced one failure after another and still became President of the United States. Thomas Edison worked tirelessly to create a better light bulb. Winston Churchill never gave up either, and remember Bill Roberts?"

"Who was Bill Roberts?" my brother asked.

"You never heard of him?" my father responded. "Well, that's because he gave up." Point made.

So you're a little lost

If you are going to be successful, you must change any negative thoughts you are having to positive thoughts. If you think something might be impossible, ask yourself these questions:

★ What can be changed or done to make it possible?

★ How can I be better tomorrow?

★ If it was possible, where would I start?

★ Who can help me make this a reality?

★ How can I do this differently in order to get the result I want?

★ What is the absolute worst possible thing that can happen if I try?

★ Can I live with that?

If you are prepared to live with the worst that can happen, you'll be able to take the risk and handle the really big challenges.

What most people don't realize is that achieving 100 percent of their goals is not a requirement. Even if you don't achieve everything, you will still be out in front of where you were. It is a fact that goals, whether they are totally achieved or not, still constructively change your life.

To try to do something really big and fail could be the best thing that ever happened to you. A wise philosopher once said, "It is far better to try mighty things and fail, than to try nothing and succeed!"

Some people subscribe to the belief there is no such thing as "try." You either do the deed or you don't. I disagree with that. I think of the word "try" as an acronym meaning "To Respect Yourself." If you don't try, you won't respect yourself. To try means you respected yourself enough to put forth some effort toward your desired result. When you do that, you will also gain the respect of others.

If we make the effort, and for some reason we don't meet our goals the first time, it doesn't mean we are a failure. Failure is when we give up the effort . . . when we stop trying. Failure is also when we don't make the effort to be all we can be! I once heard a slogan which stuck in my mind. You might want to write it down and post it somewhere you will see it often. "It matters not if you try and fail. And fail and try again. But it matters much if you try and fail. And fail *to* try again."

How far can you go?

While in junior high school, my sister wanted to be a high-jumper. She was pretty good and she jumped as high as she thought she could go. However, she would never raise the bar above a certain level because she thought that was her limit. One day her coach told her she would never know how high she could jump unless she kept raising the bar and trying to jump over it at the next level. So he raised the bar. She jumped and she knocked it down over and over again. She was very discouraged and came home crying. Mom told her to sit down, close her eyes, and see herself jump over that bar with room to spare. Mom made her practice this visualization over and over. The next day the coach raised the bar; she jumped and ultimately cleared the bar . . . with some room to spare. How will we know how far we can go if we don't keep raising the bar until we know we can go no higher? How do you know when you can go no higher? Close your eyes and see yourself doing it. See how far you can go.

Don't miss out on opportunities

Don't throw away your ideas and dreams because you are afraid or your experience is limited. I missed one of the biggest opportunities of my life because of fear. All my life I had wanted to be a model. My mom worked an extra job in order for me to go to a modeling school. I did a few modeling jobs during high school and paid for more classes. Later, my fiancé paid for more modeling lessons instead of buying an engagement ring. He gave me the choice. He could only afford one or the other. I took the modeling lessons. I practiced and practiced. One day the instructor said I could be a student model in a fashion show in the El Cortez showroom in downtown Las Vegas. When that day came, I was so scared and nervous. I was standing backstage with my instructor, who was a real professional model and featured in the fashion show, and I said to her, "I'm really scared." I was looking for some moral support, but instead she said, "I don't care and neither does anyone else. Don't say it again. Just go out there and do your best." I was so startled by the lack of caring on the part of my own personal instructor, I went out there and I did something. I'm sure it was not my best as I was about to burst into tears through all five changes.

In the future, when I got opportunities to be in shows, I never voiced my fears. My mom said to keep thinking of that little train in one of my childhood story books that said, "I think I can. I think I can." I'd stand backstage and repeat that refrain to myself over and over again. Eventually, I became a good model and an instructor. On a dare from a male model, I entered a regional modeling competition in Salt Lake City and won. The prize was an airline ticket to New York City and the opportunity to compete in the World Modeling Association "Model of the Year" competition being held there.

Because by then, I was a professional model and teaching modeling I was entered in the Career Modeling Division. I was a nervous wreck preparing for the trip to New York. Who would I be competing against? What would I wear for the competition? How would I do hair changes with each outfit in such a limited amount of time? How would I present each garment? Should I compete in runway competition only, or should I enter the photography modeling competition and the TV commercial competition as well? I decided to enter all three . . . just maybe I would place in one of them. Even if I didn't place, at least I'd have the experience.

After we arrived in New York and registered for the competition, I was one of the models selected to be in a big Easter fashion parade at the Waldorf Astoria Hotel. We were fitted for the clothing we would show, had appointments with makeup artists and hair stylists, and were required to participate in rehearsals. I was so caught up in the show, I didn't practice for the competition.

Competition day came and I got through my fifty poses for the photography competition. Next, I did the TV commercial competition.

Then came the big night — the final competition — runway techniques. All the models were in line along the side of the room, so we could watch the models competing ahead of us. I was near the end of the line. As I watched them, my mind starting playing a negative tape. The tape went like this, "Oh, she's really good. Her clothes are fantastic. I should have practiced instead of doing that show at the Waldorf. How did I let myself get distracted? Uh-oh, this one is better than the last one. Oh no, this one is beautiful and she moves so elegantly. I'll never be able to do that. I don't have a chance in this contest. I'm not as good as they are." Then another voice inside my head screamed at me, "***Quit looking at them! Quit looking at them right now!!!***" So I turned and faced the wall. As I waited and waited for my turn, looking at the wall the rest of the time, I started consciously playing a new tape in my mind. "I'm a good model. I can do this. I know how to show clothes. I have a good stage personality. I'm tall. I look good today. My hair turned out nicely. My dress is simple and elegant. It doesn't matter how I compare to others. I just have to do my best. I think I can. I think I can." I was feeling more confident. I said these affirmations over and over and over. And then it was my turn. All I had to do was be the best I could be. The audience response was positive. The judges smiled back at me.

Later in the evening, I sat in the audience waiting to hear who had won, hoping I would place somewhere in the final few. When it came to first runner-up in the overall competition and my name had not been called,

I gave up hope. I was actually getting out of my chair to leave when I heard the emcee say, "And the winner of the overall competition, with the highest number of points in every category is . . ." and there was my name, "Judi Moreo." I just stood there, frozen, until someone gave me a little push toward the stage. Then it started to sink in that I really had won. "Oh wow. I really did. This is not a dream." I heard the emcee say, "Judi will leave tomorrow for Paris, where she will represent the United States in the World Modeling Association's international competition." In my mind I immediately thought, "I can't go. I didn't bring my passport. Besides, I promised the minister at my church I would do a presentation for the youth group this week." I accepted the trophy and then blurted out to the emcee, the audience, and the world that I couldn't go to Paris. I had so programmed myself that I wasn't going, I just didn't see any other possibility and I didn't take time to think. I just said I couldn't go.

Here's how I sabotaged myself. I knew before I'd even made the trip to New York that if I should happen to win, I would have to leave the next day for Paris for the international competition. Because I didn't believe I would win, I didn't take my passport to New York. I was probably the only model there without one. To make matters worse, I opened my mouth and said, "No, I can't go." When I called my husband and told him I had won but didn't have my passport, he so wonderfully said to me, "Honey, I can airmail your passport tonight and first thing tomorrow morning I'll call the church and change your speaking date, or I'll get them someone else to fill in for you. I'm sure they'll understand." But it was too late. I had already said "No" and they had given my ticket to the first runner-up.

I missed this opportunity of a lifetime because I certainly didn't want to look like a "hopeful fool" by bringing my passport along "just in case." There was that fear of failure once again, this time disguised as the fear of looking arrogant. I sabotaged my own success and missed the opportunity to represent the United States in an international competition. I tried to appease myself by taking pride in the fact that I kept my word to the youth group, but even they were disappointed that I didn't go on to Paris. I had never even considered I could renegotiate my agreement with them.

Why did I sabotage myself? Fear. Why did I think I didn't have a chance to actually win? Not enough confidence. Was I hard on myself afterwards for allowing fear to win? You bet. Would my life have been different if I had believed in myself enough to carry my passport? Maybe. Would I have won the international competition? Maybe. Would I have felt better about myself? Most definitely. This was not the first time I experienced the fear of failure, but this was the most painful. This fear is fierce. It's unforgiving. It kicked me in the teeth and it taught me a valuable lesson. Have your passport ready and say "Yes" to all opportunities. You can always change your mind after you investigate the possibilities. You can renegotiate agreements. If you say "No" before you explore the possibilities or even give yourself a chance, you may miss the opportunity of your lifetime. I won't give into it again! I pray you won't either.

Do you want to go to Paris or don't you?

The fear of failure and the fear of rejection are intertwined. If I fail, I will be criticized and I won't get the approval of others, and therefore, I will be rejected, which in turn, will mean I failed. When we have this thinking, we go to extremes in our attempts to make others like us or approve of us. This basic fear is very real and it rules many of our lives. We let other people's opinions and disapproval rob us of our enthusiasm, our imagination, our initiative, our self-reliance, and our individuality. I even left my passport at home, so people wouldn't criticize me for wanting to go to Paris. Criticism can be one of the most destructive forces there is. It can do damage in countless ways, because it plants the seeds of fear and resentment in our hearts and in our minds.

We all know people who work tirelessly in an effort to gain acceptance. They exhaust themselves and won't rest until they are sick or in the hospital. They are unhappy with their lives and feel pressure to succeed. They are extremely driven, and unfortunately, are also very unsatisfied.

When will we learn not to be so concerned with the opinions of others? This is my life. Your life is your life. It doesn't matter what other people think if you are doing what truly makes you happy and you aren't hurting anyone else in the process. We will be successful when we have enough confidence in our own decisions to do what is right for us. Ask other people for advice and consider their opinions if you feel the need, but do what your heart tells you is right for you.

So what if you aren't keeping up with the Joneses

Madonna is not the only one who has become "a material girl in a material world." Many of us live with the fear of poverty every day. We are afraid that we won't live in the right neighborhood, drive the right car, wear the right clothes, carry the right handbag, or be able to sustain the right lifestyle. This desire for more and more is directly connected to what others will think of us. If we don't have as much as they do, they might look down their noses at us. You could go deeply into debt trying to keep up with your neighbors and friends, but there is no guarantee that having more material possessions will make you any happier . . . or even make you fit in. We have become a nation of spenders!!! Just because we want it doesn't mean we should have it! Are we buying all of these things because we are trying to fill the void of satisfaction in our lives?

Close self-scrutiny may disclose how very much we want the "right people" to think we are the right kind of person, too! Many of us are so eager to acquire material things we don't nourish our values, our health, our integrity, or our spiritual selves. Many people believe if they had all the money they needed, everything else in their lives would be fine. This is not true. Money may buy you a multitude of things, but it will not ensure that you are healthy, happy, or have great relationships. If you are sick, all the money in the world won't buy the health you desire.

Symptoms of fear of poverty

There are many symptoms of poverty consciousness. If you can recognize and eliminate these symptoms before they become ingrained as your lifestyle, you will never again have to worry about poverty. These symptoms are known as laziness, indecision, doubt, fault-finding, procrastination, complaining, and compulsive spending. Additional symptoms include a lack of ambition, a lack of self-control, and neglect of your personal appearance. If any of these symptoms have crept into your life, get rid of them right away. The longer you allow them to remain, the more consumed you become by your poverty consciousness.

Eliminate these symptoms and poverty will disappear from your mind and your life. You will find yourself in control of all you want to achieve and you will have both the relationships and possessions you desire. How much is enough? Where do you draw the line? Decide now what you really need and what you are willing to accept, and then stop beating yourself up for not having more.

You only live once

You have a right and even a responsibility to be happy. Happiness is a state of mind. Many people let life pass them by because they choose to be unhappy. They sit around complaining, worrying, procrastinating, and gossiping about other people instead of making the most of every day. They talk about the past and how it was "back when." Some of them live in the state of "one time." "One time" we did this and "one time" we did that. People who talk and think mainly about the past don't move forward. They seem to think they will repeat past happiness by reliving their old experiences. In the meantime, their real life circumstances aren't very happy. How sad that they are reminiscing about how life was "back when" and aren't living each day to its fullest now. Why aren't they trying to make themselves happy today? They don't have a clue how difficult it is for others to be around them. We've probably heard their stories a dozen times and while we weren't particularly interested the first time, we certainly didn't want to hear the same stories the third or fourth time. These people don't really have any concern for whether their stories are interesting to us or not. They are talking because they want to relive their experiences.

Other people talk about "someday when." "Someday when" I make a lot of money, "someday when" I meet the right person, "someday when" my kids are out of school. But "someday when" comes and there's another "someday when" holding them back. Maybe you are one of these people. If you've ever glorified the future believing when something changes, everything else will be better, then you are guilty of living in the future. If your household income is $35,000 a year and you talk about how wonderful life will be as soon as you are earning $50,000 a year, you need to stop right now. You are kidding yourself. By the time you earn $50,000 per year, you will want or need $75,000. Your material desires will always outgrow and outpace your income, especially if you are looking to BUY your happiness. The truth is, if you are not happy with yourself, no amount of money will change things. There will always be someone who earns more than you, has more than you, and spends more than you. Projecting your life into the future is a way of avoiding the present . . . not taking responsibility for now.

This is very similar to the state of "if only." "If only" I were thin, "if only" I had more money, "if only" I had a better education, and the ultimate declaration: "If only" I'd win the lottery. Wishing and waiting are not powerful. They will not bring the changes you seek. My feeling is "if only" you'd concentrate on what you can do today to take the steps toward what you want to be, do, and have, you'd be a lot happier. You'd be achieving and accomplishing what you want, **and** you'd be enjoying the journey as well. Whenever we spend too much time in the past or the future, life seems to slip by before we ever accomplish what we want.

Learn to balance your thinking and your conversation

We all have a past, a present, and a future. Talking about the past can be wonderful if your stories are affirming, colorful, or pleasant, positive memories. Through the sharing of experiences and knowledge, we can build quality relationships.

Talking about the future can be good as long as you focus on your goals . . . what you want to be, do, and have. When you talk about your future goals, be sure you are talking to someone who will support you. It's hard to accept that sometimes even those who love us may try to discourage us. They don't intend to inflict their negative attitudes on us, but their good intentions of not wanting to see us try something and fail comes through as disapproval or discouragement. Be sure to share your goals with those who have done what you want to do. They will tell you how they did it and maybe even offer assistance. Many successful people enjoy becoming a mentor to someone who seeks their advice. If you talk to someone who has never done what you want to do, that person will tell you all the reasons you can't do it, why it won't happen, and even why it's impossible to achieve.

Talking about the present is a wonderful way to "share the moment." When we are fully present or "in the moment," we are better listeners and display more interest in others, making them feel more important. When we are in the moment, we are at our best. English professor, John Keating, Robin Williams' character in the movie, *Dead Poets Society*, memorably pointed out how important it is to, "Seize the day." So many people miss the experience of the moment because they are dwelling on the past or the future.

If others with whom you are speaking insist on changing the conversation back to the "one time–when we–if only" mode, then ask a question or make a statement to change the direction of the conversation toward the present. Learn to take control of the negative situations in your life and you will soon find that your friends and family will stop coming to you to commiserate about how awful things are. If you don't give them the reinforcement they are looking for when they are attempting to share their misery with you, they'll look elsewhere for someone who will.

In addition, ask your friends to help you by pointing out to you those times when you get into this mode. They will appreciate being given permission to change the energy of the conversation from time to time.

Quit making potholes into canyons

Stop worrying about little things and get on with your life. Our beliefs determine our successes in life. The minister at my church once told me, "Worry is a form of prayer and the form most people practice most often." I'm sure he didn't mean to be negative, but he wanted me to realize what people focus on is what they bring about. Worry is fear. Worry is a state of mind which is brought about by indecision. Everything in your life begins with an idea. If you have the idea something will go wrong, it will. Make a decision to give up fear. Know that all things ultimately work out for the best and this will bring you peace of mind, calmness, and power. You will be able to think more rationally when you are at peace.

Life isn't always easy

Who told you life was going to be easy? There are lots of troubles, irritations, and pains in life. Things happen. Things go wrong. People don't always do what we want them to. Don't depend on other people for your happiness. Depend on yourself. Be who you are. Do the things you want to do. Get for yourself the things you want to have. Don't wait for someone else to be it, do it, or get it for you. The only places you will find knights in shining armor on white horses are in shows on the Las Vegas Strip and in old black-and-white movies. No one is going to ride up and save you. Take care of your own needs. It is not selfish to take care of yourself. The *Bible* says "to love thy neighbor **as** thyself." It doesn't say "***instead of*** thyself." This is called self-reliance. Learn the difference between wishing, hoping, and desiring. Desire is a motivating force. When you desire something enough and back it up with hard work, you will make it come alive in your life.

Successful people understand there is a price to pay for achieving success. Sometimes this involves making sacrifices in order to reach your goals. My dad used to remind me often, "People are successful because they do the things failures don't like and are not willing to do. Successful people take full responsibility for finding their own path to achievement."

Many setbacks are foreseeable

If we take the time to think about what possible obstacles will come up, we can be prepared to take alternative action. Be prepared by asking yourself, "How would I handle this situation if I run into a roadblock or if an emergency occurs?" No matter what your situation, you can make your journey easier if you prepare yourself by exploring the alternative routes in advance.

Unforeseeable circumstances

Recently, I was the keynote speaker at the Blind Merchants Association Convention. The organizer of the event asked me if I would attend the Women's Breakfast the next morning and maybe say a few words about entrepreneurship. I eagerly agreed to do so.

I don't know what I expected, but I didn't expect the hotel to serve a buffet-style meal for a group of blind women. I watched in absolute awe as these women with guide dogs and canes successfully maneuvered the buffet line, serving themselves and carrying their plates to their respective tables to sit down and eat. It was the sort of task that even a sighted person might have trouble maneuvering.

The speaker before me was an attorney. As I listened to her flawless presentation, I marveled at the thought of her going through all those years of school and study to become an attorney without being able to see. It's hard enough to pass the bar exam when you have your sight.

Losing one's eyesight is an unforeseeable circumstance, but these women don't let it hold them back. They run successful businesses and attend national conventions, where they discuss the various trials and tribulations they experience daily as women entrepreneurs and focus on possible solutions. Being a part of this incredible experience made me realize that many of us take our abilities and blessings for granted. Sure, we have unforeseeable circumstances, but most of them are minor compared to losing your eyesight. The big lesson I learned that day was, "You don't have to be able to see to have vision."

Successful people see something in their imagination, desire it enough to set goals, prepare, plan, and then take action to get it. The action part is the key. You can set goals, prepare, and plan forever, but if you don't take some action, absolutely nothing will happen.

Which path will you take?

You will never accomplish the things you want if you keep telling yourself that you can't . . . that you don't have the money, the resources, the contacts, the education, or the self-confidence.

We all have self-confidence. Some of us are confident we will be successful. Others of us are confident we will be failures. Whichever it is, our confidence determines the path we travel. Make up your mind. Which will it be?

Negativity is a virus

We are all susceptible to the negative influences of others and we must protect ourselves. Negativity strikes in many forms. You can catch it. If someone around you is negative and complains a lot, you may soon find yourself griping and complaining as well. Or you may find yourself feeling disappointed about life. It's possible that you may even become depressed. You may start to doubt your abilities and give up on your dreams. Negativity often comes disguised as "good advice" or "realistic objectivity." When people who care about you discourage you or point out what is wrong with your ideas, it's usually because they are trying to protect you from being hurt. They don't understand the negative result of their good intentions.

You must realize these seemingly caring words of caution from your family and friends are actually negative influences that work through your subconscious. They trigger old feelings of insecurity and doubt. You will need to protect yourself by building up your "emotional immune system." Stay away from people who are habitually negative, no matter how well-intended they seem. Build up relationships with people who are positive, supportive, and inspiring. Learn to deal with criticism. Listen, evaluate the source and accuracy, and then respond. Don't accept it, avoid it, ignore it, or attempt to defend yourself against it. Your best response is, "I'll take that into consideration." If you buy into their negativity, you are likely to stay stuck exactly where you are or even end up in worse circumstances. Consider whether or not there are any constructive ideas in what they say which will help you improve your attitude, your communication, your behavior, or your life and let go of the rest.

Be creative about your future

Don't think for a moment that you aren't creative. You are creating your life right now, one day at a time. So why not create the life you want? Everything you need to make your life what you want it to be already exists. What you must do is look at what you have and what's around you. Then, figure out how to rearrange things from the way they are to the way you want them to be. Norman Monath said, "The only time to settle for things as they are is when what they are is exactly what you want."

Do you have vision?

Can you see where you are going? Do you have a vision set firmly in your mind of how you want your life to be? Are you making the best of where you are now, in order to get where you want to go? Do you love your job? Your relationships? Your home? Your physique? Your lifestyle? Are you truly grateful for all you do and have? Are you making the most of your talents, skills, and abilities? Are you happy with yourself? If not, you are the only one who can do anything about it. Your happiness is your responsibility. Don't blame the company where you work, your boss, your family, the city, the traffic, the weather, the car manufacturer, the oil company, or anyone else for your unhappiness.

Webster's dictionary defines happiness as, "a state of well-being and pleasurable satisfaction." For me, happiness is doing what I love to do with people I enjoy being around. Happiness is being able to use my talent, skills, and abilities to make a difference in the lives of others.

We demonstrate happiness by being cheerful, joyful, optimistic, or content. The very demonstration of happiness brings more happiness. Happiness is a state of mind. You make a decision to do the things you need to do in order to make yourself happy. Abraham Lincoln once said, "A man is about as happy as he makes up his mind to be."

Your success is waiting

Life is an adventure to be lived. Today is a new beginning. Imagine the exciting things you can do, the wonderful relationships you can have, the places you can go, and who you can be when you give up your fear. Choose success. It's just as easy . . . if not easier . . . than failure. Based on my experiences, I can tell you that success certainly feels the better of the two. Choose success and you'll never look back with regret.

You will have more *purpose, passion,* and *power* when you decide to take total responsibility for who you are and the choices you make. Your success is waiting for you. Claim it!

Possibilities Exercise

Go to your favorite quiet place or anywhere you can feel comfortable and relaxed. Allow yourself to dream about possibilities. When you feel relaxed, list below all of the things you would like to do and have as well as places you would like to go.

1. _____

_____

_____

_____

2. _____

_____

_____

_____

3. _____

_____

_____

_____

4. _____

_____

_____

_____

5. _____

_____

_____

_____

6. _____

_____

_____

_____

7. _____

_____

_____

_____

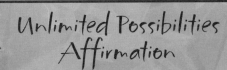

Unlimited Possibilities Affirmation

I am awakened to the unlimited possibilities to be lived. I erase my boundaries and embrace new adventures. I reach beyond the horizon to a fuller, richer life. I am more than enough.

Chapter Three

Choose Your Future

You can have anything you want if you want it desperately enough. You must want it with an inner exuberance that erupts through the skin and joins the energy that created the world.

— SHEILAH GRAHAM, AMERICAN GOSSIP COLUMNIST

If you had all the money you would need, all the time it would take, and you knew you absolutely couldn't fail, what would you do? Who would you do it with? Where would you go? What would you have? What would you want to be? In other words, what goals would you set for yourself, if you knew you couldn't fail?

Deciding all these things is what I call vision-setting. If the world was perfect and money was no object, this is the picture you hold in your mind of who and what you would be, what you would do and have, and where you would go. In vision-setting, we put this picture in our minds as though it is happening to us right now. We hold it there. If you will do this, your subconscious mind will find a way to make these things happen, in spite of the facts that the world isn't perfect and money may be an issue.

There are many people in the world who have great talents and still haven't succeeded. Talent is not the essential ingredient for getting what you want or becoming the person you want to be. Talent helps, but you and I both know talented people who don't use their talents to better their lives.

Being in control of your life is a choice

Many of us think we have no control over our lives. Failure to accomplish what we want in life is a result of failing to believe in ourselves enough. We let doubt sneak in and then we make excuses about our abilities, time constraints, training, and talents. Doubt creates stress, panic, and anxiety. These defeat our plans and goals.

Sometimes people succeed in a conventional sense, but lack happiness because they aren't doing what they really want. Instead, they attempt to fulfill the desires and goals of someone else rather than their own. Perhaps they have fallen under the influence of a parent or a spouse. How can they feel passionate about something they don't really want? They have probably even stopped making any effort toward their real goals, because of a fear of failure, a fear of rejection, or a lack of self-worth. If only they would pursue their own interests and use their natural talents, they would be sure to succeed.

Joe is a very talented performer and artist. He could have been a major star in either field, but he married a woman who threw temper tantrums every time he mentioned investing in his career. He needed promotional photos and demo records, but she felt there were more important things like designer jeans, sculptured fingernails and having her hair colored by the most expensive hairdresser in town. She nagged at him constantly about getting a "real job" to support her, her kids, and his kids. She didn't work outside the home. She felt it was his responsibility to bring in the money for all the things they needed, including a swimming pool, which, of course, was a necessity for their neighborhood. He gave up performing and got a job as a beverage manager in a casino hotel. This seemed easier than listening to her daily moaning and misery. He hated the new job, but he brought home a regular paycheck. His wife continued to spend. Oddly enough, she found something new to complain about. He wasn't home enough. They both became more and more unhappy as they got more and more in debt. Eventually, they divorced. As it turned out, neither of them got what they wanted and his true talents were wasted for all those years.

There is a happy ending to this story . . . at least for one of them. After their divorce, he quit the job he hated and went back to doing what he loves. Today he is a commercial artist, and three nights a week he entertains at a very nice dinner club. He has a new wife who is supportive of him and what he loves. The best part, he is happy.

A reason to get up

When we know what we want and take action in the direction of our goals, it gives us a reason to get up in the morning. When the goal is our own and we work toward it, we have more energy and our days become exciting.

Think about how much time you have left to live, if you live to the average life expectancy, which is about 77 years. How old are you now? How much time do you have left to finally live your life the way you want to live? We are all born into greatness and through our upbringing or life circumstances, we sometimes allow life to pull us down into mediocrity. It's not necessary. Decide now how you want to spend your time. If you are feeling like life is passing you by and you don't feel a burning passion inside of you urging you to fulfill your life's purpose, then something is wrong! Ask yourself these questions:

★   When was I the happiest in my life?

★   What things made me happy?

★   How much time do I spend now doing the things I like to do most?

★   How often do I feel that I am not accomplishing anything?

Then:

★   Make a list of what your childhood dreams were.

★   Make a list of your wishes as they are now.

★   Make a list of all the things that you do well.

★   Make a list of all the things you'd like to do.

Once you have analyzed yourself, you will have an idea of what's missing, what's needed, and what's next!

Determine the destination

Start now to establish concrete goals for yourself within the framework of your true talents and interests. Determine what your needs, wants, and desires are — for now and for the future. You can't gain control over your life without knowing which direction you want to go and having a plan of action to get you there. Goals focus your energies in one direction ... toward your vision. Defining your goals will put your imagination to work. You will start to concentrate on what you really want, rather than just getting by day after day. When you decide what you want in specific detail, then your mind will start to formulate a plan to make it happen. Define your goals!

If you don't know where you want to go, you'll end up wandering around lost, getting nowhere. The majority of people have only a clue as to what they really want to do or be. They say they want to be happier, travel, or be rich. What does that mean? Happier than what? Travel where? And what is rich? These goals are different for different people. For someone earning minimum wage, rich might be earning $34,000 a year. For someone earning $100,000, being rich might mean earning millions. You must be specific when you are setting your vision and mapping out your goals. Do you want to have enough money so you never have to worry about money again? How much is enough? Do you want to travel around the world or only to places with warm climates? Which one is it? Do you like boating, skiing, and horseback riding? Or would you rather give big dinner parties? Do you want to find your soul mate? Perhaps you want to send your children to the best schools so they can have great careers. Or maybe you would just like to take them to the park on Sunday for a picnic. Happiness and success are different things to different people. You must first decide what your vision is and then set your goals. If you don't know where you want to go, you won't get anywhere.

A few years ago, I moved to South Africa where they drive on the other side of the road. The steering wheel is on the right side of the car, with the car physically sitting to the left of the driver's body. In the United States, I know as well as anyone where the *right* side of my car is. Well, in South Africa, everything is reversed. It was really difficult to judge how much space the *left* side of my car took up! Consequently, I hit things ... like posts, gates, cars, and motorcycles, so I decided to go to work earlier in the day and come home later at night. This way, I would encounter less traffic, and hopefully, have a much safer drive. I worked out a route from my home to work and back that would take me about 20 minutes each way without the rush hour traffic.

On my way home from work one night, however, there was road construction and I had to get off my chosen path. I became very confused and got lost. I stopped several times at service stations and cafes and asked for directions, but no one seemed to know the suburb where I lived. I eventually made it home after four and a half hours. It really was a miracle that I found my way home at all. You can imagine my emotional state!

At work the next day, I mentioned to Marietta, the Afrikaans lady with whom I worked, that it had taken me four and a half hours to get home. She asked me where I lived. I told her "Hou Links," pronouncing it "How Links." She said she had never heard of it. I told her I had asked several other people and no one else had heard of it either. Then she asked me how to spell it . . . so I spelled out H-O-U L-I-N-K-S. She stared at me blankly for a few minutes and then said, "Why do you think you live there?" I replied that there was a sign near my house that looked like our suburb signs in America and that's what it said. It also had the suburb's slogan underneath. Well, she started to laugh. "Judi, that's not a suburb sign. And it's not pronounced 'How Links.' It's 'Ho Links.' It's not where you live; it means 'Keep Left.' That writing underneath is not the slogan. It says, 'Slower traffic, keep to the right.'"

I'm sharing this story with you so you will realize that I know firsthand if you don't know where you are going, you may not get where you want to go. . . . You'll just keep wandering around hoping to find what you want. If you want to get somewhere in life you need to determine, ahead of time, where you want to end up. The journey becomes clear when the destination is known.

Set goals that will motivate and inspire you

You need to know what you want. In goal-setting, it's okay to be selfish! Do you have any childhood dreams that remain unfulfilled or any cities that you have always wanted to see, but never visited? Consider all the material things you want, the lifestyle you desire, the places you would like to go, or things you would like to do and incorporate them into your goals. What is important to you? What are your most important values? When do you feel most needed and appreciated? What do you love to do? What gets you excited? What would you like your tombstone to say?

I remember the day my dad had me sit down at the kitchen table and asked me that question: "What would you like your tombstone to say?" My first thought was, "What have I done now to make him want to kill me?"

It wasn't anything I had done. He wanted me to write down how I would like to be remembered and to put that piece of paper in my wallet and a copy on my bathroom mirror. He said, "If you will always hold this thought in the forefront of your mind, it will be like a compass, always keeping you on your true path in life. It will make your choices easier, because you will always remember where you want to go and not choose to take detours that present themselves disguised as opportunities."

He elaborated, "The grass often looks greener somewhere else, but it doesn't matter how green the grass is, if it's not located where we want to go."

Write down your goals

Set definite goals for things you want to have and to do. Write down that dream you have been carrying around in your head. Don't believe any desire is too great or out-of-reach. Be descriptive. Writing down your goals will help you acknowledge them, commit to them, and then act on them. When you put your goals in writing, add every detail. Describe your new home's square footage and its location. Write down the length and name of that new boat you've always wanted. Finally, use positive phrases. Instead of "I want a new home" write "I will be enjoying my new beach house by . . . (write in a specific date).

Goal-setting is what we do for ourselves

Be honest with yourself. Don't write down things you think you should want. Don't write down things other people have told you to want. Goal-setting is not something we do to please others. Write down only what you want. You will spend a lot of time achieving your goal, so make it meaningful and fun. Then write down what you are willing to do to get it.

Self-motivation

You probably aren't even aware of how easy it will be to achieve your goals when you start to believe you can and then take steps in the direction of your goals. Action is what it will take to make your goals a reality. Writing them down is your first action. Then you will need to focus on the goals and work toward them . . . one step at a time. Don't worry about knowing all the steps at the beginning. Just start. With each step, you'll see how to go further and that will increase your self-motivation.

Self-motivation is the bridge between thinking about your goals and accomplishing them. Self-motivation is the desire you have to achieve or obtain something. It is essential to have if we are to succeed in any endeavor. It isn't something that comes naturally for everyone. It can be learned and developed. It is the inner desire that keeps us always moving forward in spite of discouragement, mistakes, and setbacks.

You can build this desire and achieve your goals by staying forward-focused and allowing only positive thoughts to dominate your thinking. You must believe you are a success for success to come your way.

Planning your future

Set goals in the eight major areas of your life:

★ Career	★ Finances	
★ Health	★ Relationships	
★ Recreation	★ Education	
★ Community	★ Spiritual	

Each area of your life should be planned, keeping in mind how you will achieve the goals you are setting. Write steps or sub-goals to use as checkpoints, so you will be able to tell whether or not you are making progress. Ask yourself questions that pertain to each area of your life. The answers will define your direction and goals. Once you begin, you will be amazed at how quickly things start to happen for you.

At the end of this chapter, I have designated a place for you to list what you want to happen in each of the eight areas of your life. What do you want to have, be, and do with your life ten or fifteen years from now?

Career

Do you enjoy the work you are doing now? Are you happy where you are? Or is there something else you'd rather be doing? Do you want a higher or different position? Are you using your talents fully in your current position? Is there a better place for your talents and abilities? What skills do you need to develop if you're doing something now that isn't making you happy? What kind of money do you want to earn? How would you plan your day if you had a choice? What obstacles are preventing you from achieving your ideal day? Are you willing to make the effort to achieve professional excellence?

Finances

What are you doing now to prepare for your future? Would you like to make more money? How much money do you want to have? What will you do with it? Will you buy property or securities? Will you make other investments? Do you want to keep your money in a savings account? Do you want or need business capital or an education fund? Do you have enough money saved so that if you had a serious illness or setback you could continue your lifestyle for at least six months without worry? When will you take charge of your financial well-being?

Health

How healthy do you want to be? What physical fitness program do you have? If you don't have one, what would you like to do and when will you start? How much do you want to weigh? Do you want or need to eat differently? Would you like to play a sport, join a walking group, hire a personal trainer, or take a dance class? When will you begin?

Relationships

What condition are your relationships in? Which relationships do you want to maintain? How would you like your relationship with your spouse or significant other to be? With your children? With your parents? With other relatives? What activities would you like to share with your family? What will you change and when?

Recreation

What do you consider recreation? What does "fun" mean to you? Who would you play with? Would you like to be involved in some kind of association or theater group? Would you like to take art lessons? Play golf? Picnic at the lake? Water-ski? Snow-ski? Visit a national park? Go to the zoo? When will you do it? How will you look and dress when you are having fun?

Education

What would you like to study? What would happen as a result of educating yourself? What would you like to read? Are there classes you want to take? Where would you take them? Would you rather travel and learn about other cultures? Where would you go? What would you see? Would you learn a new language? When will you take steps to make this happen? What will be your first step?

Community

How will you get involved? What service organizations might be of interest to you? Do you want to be a volunteer? Do you want to run for political office? Or serve on a committee? Would you like to Adopt-A-Highway? Clean up the community? Coach a neighborhood sports team? Serve as a scout leader? Host an educational television show on a public broadcast station? When will you make time to do this?

Spiritual

What are you striving for spiritually? Do you want to attend religious services? Volunteer at your place of worship? Read religious publications? Would you prefer to spend time in meditation or prayer? Would you like to be a more loving person? Serve someone who is in need? When will you take time to do this for yourself?

SMART Goals

Once you have given considerable time and thought to the evaluation of your life, you will have the vision and the big picture. Big picture dreams are wonderful. They inspire and excite. It's up to you. It is now time to turn your dreams, intentions, and desires into firm, achievable goals. Writing out your goals, using the **SMART** method — **S**pecific,

Measurable, **A**greed-upon, **R**ealistic, and **T**ime-framed — is the first step to living your dreams. **SMART** goals make it easy to stay on track and resist temptation that may attempt to sidetrack you in directions you don't want to go.

Specific

Be very specific when writing your goals. Detail every aspect. Writing down your specific goals clarifies exactly where you are going and how you will know when you have arrived. Assess where you are now in relation to where you want to go. By evaluating your current position, you will be able to measure the distance between where you are and your destination. This will enable you to write sub-goals for the steps you will need to take. Also, you can identify changes you may want to make along the way. Take a close look at your current title, income, residence - anything that may change in reaching your goals. With a realistic assessment of your current situation, you will be better able to set achievable goals.

Measurable

Regular assessment is how you measure progress. Set a timeline and determine checkpoints in order to keep track of your progression toward your goal. Remember, big visions take time to materialize. Identify several smaller goals you must accomplish to reach your big one. As you reach each small goal, reward yourself and move on to the next. It is important to celebrate your successes as you go. Recognizing your achievements along the way will help you keep a positive attitude throughout the journey.

Measurement is how we keep track of our progress and how we know if and when we begin to veer off the charted path. In this way, we can immediately make any needed adjustments.

Agreed upon

If there are other people whose cooperation you need in order to reach your goal, you need to get their agreement early in the journey. If they don't agree to do their part or to support you in achieving your goals, your journey will be more difficult than it need be, or it may not be attainable at all.

Realistic

When your goals aren't realistic, you are setting yourself up to fail before you have even started. Your goals must be high enough to motivate you and still be realistic. If you don't believe they are realistic, self-doubt will set in and undermine you, causing you to become immobilized. Ask yourself if your goals will create conflict in any other areas of your life. How far are you willing to go to get what you want?

Ascertaining what you want requires self-examination to determine the extent to which your skills, beliefs, values, and attitudes relate to your objectives. You will be more likely to succeed if your objectives evolve from your natural abilities and a positive attitude. Achieving your goals requires a high sense of priority that will require belief and discipline. Make sure you have given yourself realistic time frames and any resources you may need. Don't be concerned with how realistic these goals appear to anyone else. Just be sure you believe you can do what you have set out to do.

I learned a valuable lesson from a speaking colleague by the name of Jerry Traylor. Jerry told a group of his friends that he had two goals: one was to run a marathon and the other was to climb Pikes Peak. Many people attempted to discourage Jerry, because he has cerebral palsy, and they thought he'd never be able to achieve his goals. You may have read about Jerry in the newspaper or on the Internet. He did run his marathon . . . from San Francisco to New York City, 3,528 miles in seven months. He averaged 15 miles per day and wore out two-dozen pairs of running shoes and three pairs of crutches. Along the way, Jerry delivered about two hundred motivational speeches and raised a very, very large sum of money for charity. He also attained his goal of climbing Pikes Peak . . . not once, but three times.

What I learned from Jerry was this: "It doesn't matter if your goals are realistic in anyone else's mind. Your goals must be realistic in your mind." Jerry knew he'd be able to do what he set out to do, because he was committed to a purpose. He told me he wanted to become a motivational speaker and tell people that all things are possible if they would give themselves a chance and try. "To be effective, though," he said, "I felt I'd have to establish myself as a motivational doer, if anyone was to believe what I said as a motivational speaker. I don't think anything I do is really remarkable. What's remarkable is life. I just live life and make the best of every single thing the Lord has given me to use. I just keep trying. I don't worry about falling down. And believe me, there were plenty of times when I fell flat on my face." Jerry may have fallen down, but he always got back up, because his goals were realistic and achievable to him and as Paul Harvey said at the end of his interview with Jerry, "That's the rest of the story."

Time-Framed

If you don't have a time designated as to when you will accomplish your goal, you probably won't accomplish it at all. If it doesn't matter when it gets done, it usually doesn't get done. Start your plan with the final objective and work backwards, making sure to allow enough time for each step. Knowing not only what we intend to accomplish, but when we want to accomplish it keeps us focused, as well as letting us know if we are ahead or behind our intended schedule. Timelines are set as a means of breaking projects down into smaller, bite-sized chunks, so we don't feel overwhelmed. They are not meant to stress us out or make us feel guilty. They are observable criteria that ensure our steady progress rather than leaving it to chance. Good intentions are nice, but a good plan is powerful and a timeline is essential to your success.

Get a clear picture

Cut pictures out of magazines of the things you want to have and the places you want to go. Paste the pictures next to your written goals or some place where you will see them daily to imprint them on your mind. Affirm positively, out loud, that you will achieve them.

List the benefits

It is important to identify the benefits you will derive from attaining your goal. Make a list of any way you will benefit from each of your goals, either during the process or after attainment. Focus on your rewards. Why should you be motivated? What positive consequences will you enjoy when you put your plan in motion? Visualize the rewards that achieving your goals will bring. Visualize clearly and vividly. Make it such a clear picture that you'll do almost anything to be a part of it. When you drive toward that image, you are motivated.

Leave your comfort zone behind

If staying in your comfort zone hasn't brought you the success you want, maybe it's time you stepped out of it. When you set goals, you are no longer leaving your future to chance. You are actually choosing to make changes in your life. Be prepared to feel a little uneasy at the prospect of doing things you haven't done before, and give yourself time to adjust to new situations. When we do things we haven't done before or attempt things we've only dreamed of, we often feel fears ... fear of getting lost, fear of not knowing what to do, fear of looking stupid, fear that we are not "good enough," fear of rejection and many more. It's natural to feel fear. Identify and understand your fears. Only then will you be able to defeat them. Recall job changes, moves, or other upheavals you have experienced in the past to remind yourself you adjusted then and you can adjust now as well. Take action. Action cures fear. Once you begin doing something, it becomes easier and your fears disappear. Take changes one day at a time and stay positive by focusing on the reason for them. When you are able to cope with changes, whether you make the choice to change or the changes come unexpectedly, you are taking charge of your life and your future. Before long, you will find that your comfort zone has expanded.

Set priorities

Stephen Covey said it best in his book, *The Seven Habits of Highly Effective People*, "Habit #3, First Things First." He told us we should always do the most important things first. If you will plan your days and your activities, ranking tasks in order of importance and taking care of the most important things first, you will have fewer crises in your life and you'll get more results. Priorities are also a psychological trigger to action. If you don't have pre-set priorities for your day, you could spend your entire day trying to figure out what to do next, as well as allowing anyone and everyone to interrupt you and keep you from accomplishing anything important. You may also appear disorderly and indecisive.

With clear-cut priorities, you can get your day off to a fast start and stay on the right path throughout the day, gaining momentum as you go.

Sir Isaac Newton formulated the laws that govern momentum: "A body at rest stays at rest," and "A body in motion stays in motion." It is far easier to keep working once you are on a roll than it is to get started in the first place. With your priority list, when you finish one task you will move right into the next. It will be easier to make decisions as well, because if it's not on the list, it doesn't need to be done until the priorities are finished.

People who set priorities usually accomplish more in shorter periods of time. This allows them to avoid workaholic behavior and live a quality life.

Identify possible obstacles

If you have big goals you will probably face some adversity along the way. Make a list of any people, habits, or other obstacles that may stand between you and your goals. Then decide how you will handle them. In addition to the obstacles you recognize now, consider potential changes and what obstacles those changes may present. Find out what resources are available to help you overcome obstacles. Consider opportunities for training, learning, or acquiring new technology as well as meeting and networking with new people. Take advantage of any opportunities. The road to your goals may not always be smooth, but the bumps and potholes you foresee will be easier to overcome than the ones you don't expect.

Review your goals regularly

The things you do every day will either take you closer to your goals or lead you away from them. Discipline yourself daily to do the things that need to be done to accomplish your goals. If you are going to be successful, you must stay focused on your vision. Be sure to post a written version or a picture of that vision in a place where you will see it often. Review your goals frequently in order to stay motivated. Look at the pictures you have in your book and record in your journal each day what you have done that day to accomplish your goals. As you review your goals, measure your progress and make any changes necessary in your strategy. You become what you think about, so make a mental picture of each of your goals and carry them around with you.

A lesson from an architect

Wallace Palmer, an architect in the Denver area, told me that before he starts on a project, he has an exact picture in his mind of what the building will look like. He draws a picture and makes a model of the building or project he envisions. The model has all the details right down to the landscaping. He takes pictures of the model to show others how the finished project will look and eventually a blueprint is drawn up of the most efficient way to build it.

Each of us should have an exact picture of what we want, a sense of direction, and a model, as well as a plan for making it happen. If you will translate your personal and professional wishes into goals and then pursue them with passion, you will be rewarded by the fulfillment of your potential as well as your dreams.

Just Do it!

Start now. Don't wait until you have the perfect circumstances. There will never be a time that is "exactly right." Nike has the right idea with their slogan, "Just do it!" Get in motion as soon as possible. If you have a habit of procrastinating, now is the time to break it. Act now! Stand up to your fear. Take the first step toward the first goal on your list. As your momentum builds, so will your motivation. Keep your timelines in mind to remind yourself time is ticking away. Don't make excuses for waiting and putting things off. When you have fear, you may feel frozen. This is when you should "Just do it." Take some action. The price of inaction is high, so never put off until tomorrow what you can get done today. Do something toward your goals. They will never become a reality if you don't take the first step. Action is the key to taking control.

Translate your personal and professional wishes into goals today. Align your goals with your purpose, pursue your vision with passion, and soon you will *know* that you *can't* fail, because you have unlimited possibilities and the power to choose your future.

Choosing Your Future Exercise

Write at least one goal for each of the eight major areas of your life using the guidelines you found in this chapter. Paste a picture of the goal or goals next to what you have written.

Career

_____

_____

_____

_____

_____

_____

_____

Finances

_____

_____

_____

_____

_____

_____

_____

Health

_____

_____

_____

_____

_____

_____

_____

Relationships

_____

_____

_____

_____

_____

_____

_____

Recreation

_____

_____

_____

_____

_____

_____

Education

_____

_____

_____

_____

_____

_____

Community

_____

_____

_____

_____

_____

_____

_____

_____

Spiritual

_____

_____

_____

_____

_____

_____

_____

_____

The Future Is What I Choose Affirmation

Leaving fear behind, I step out of my comfort zone and follow my vision of who I am. Clarity of purpose and the drive of passion give me the power to create the future I desire. I am confident. I am ready. I am more than enough.

Chapter Four

Imagine You Are There

When you see the invisible, you can do the impossible.

— **ORAL ROBERTS**, MINISTER AND AUTHOR

When you were a child, did you ever imagine yourself as a princess, a cowgirl, a white rabbit, a doctor, an astronaut, or another character? I did. I would transform myself into a particular character for a period of time and have a wonderful adventure. Sometimes I even imagined friends and younger brothers and sisters. My mother was taken aback when one of the ladies from the church called to find out how the new baby was that I had told her about. I had failed to add the part about the baby being imaginary.

You can use this same skill today. Imagine yourself being the person you want to become. Shakespeare said, "Assume a virtue if you have it not." In other words, act the part. Just imagine you are the person you would like to be and it won't be long until you realize you are. "Oh sure," you say, "That sounds easy. Who are you kidding?" I can just hear you.

The subconscious mind

The subconscious part of our minds causes us to feel and act in agreement with what we imagine to be true about ourselves and our environment. When we realize our behaviors are a result of the images and beliefs our minds create, we free ourselves to use our imaginations as though our thoughts are reality. If we see ourselves performing a certain way, our subconscious mind perceives we are actually performing that way. The subconscious doesn't know the difference between what is real and what is imagined. It only knows what we tell it. We can think ourselves into success and prosperity by concentrating on the good we have now and focusing on a positive future. Whatever thoughts you hold in your conscious mind give direction to your subconscious. Whatever you impress on your subconscious mind will be what you experience in your life. William James, the father of American psychology, said, "The power to move the world is in your subconscious mind."

One person who has proven this to be true is a man whom I was fortunate enough to meet while living in South Africa. I was in Cape Town in 1990 when Nelson Mandela was released after 27 years of imprisonment. I was present when he gave his State of the Union address. At a dinner we both attended at the Sowetan newspaper, I had the opportunity to speak with him. I was so impressed with this man who became President of South Africa I later bought his book, *A Long Walk to Freedom*. I read it cover-to-cover in order to learn the details of his quest. In the book, he talked about creative visualization, which he referred to as his vision of the future. He wrote, "I never seriously considered the possibility that I would not emerge from prison one day. I am fundamentally an optimist. Whether that comes from nature or nurture, I cannot say. Part of being optimistic is keeping one's head pointed toward the sun, one's feet moving forward. There were many dark moments when my faith in humanity was sorely tested, but I could not give myself up to despair. I thought continually of the day when I would walk free. Over and over, I fantasized about what I would like to do."

What did this man know that filled him with determined optimism not experienced by other men?

During my stay in South Africa, I had two opportunities to visit the cell at Robben Island where Mr. Mandela had been incarcerated. It was three paces wide and six long, with no bathroom facilities. There was just a pot in the corner and a tired, little cot on which to sleep. As I stood in that cell, I wondered if under those circumstances you and I could have chosen to believe that one day we would make the dream of freedom come true. I lived in South Africa throughout Mandela's reign as President. I watched and experienced his vision of a peaceful transition become reality. A person with less vision would never have been able to make this happen for an entire country.

Our circumstances are not as extreme as Mandela's. Certainly, if he could imagine freedom for the people of a nation and have it come true, we should be able to imagine the successful future we desire.

Creative visualization

Whenever we create something, we create it first in our minds as thoughts. As a young girl, my mother taught me to sew. First, we would go to the fabric store and select a picture from the pattern book of the garment I would like to have. We would get the pattern and read the instructions on the back to see how much fabric it would take to make this particular garment, as well as what other notions we would need. Then we would go through the store and select a fabric, trim, such as lace or ribbon, some buttons, as well as thread and a zipper. I would get so excited. I could see that garment made with that fabric before it was even cut out. I could see me wearing it and how happy I was going to be. Then we would go home, lay the pattern on the fabric, pin the pattern down, cut the fabric, pin it together and sew it up. In hardly any time at all, I would have a new dress! In fact, the more excited I was about it, the sooner the dress would get finished.

That's how ***creative visualization*** works in your life. First, you get the picture in your mind. Get clear on the outcome you desire. Vividly imagine it. You imagine what color and how big it is going to be, what supplies or resources you will need to have, if there is to be any trim, and how it fits your lifestyle. You must be able to see it in your mind in complete detail and feel it in your very being. Consciously holding this picture in your mind, your imagination goes to work on the "how to" part of the equation and will bring to your conscious mind a logical approach for making it a reality.

Once you have the vision, you are ready to start making your action plan, exploring your possibilities, and setting your goals.

Prepare yourself

Whether it is a creative endeavor like sewing or a stressful event in your life, you can prepare yourself for it by imagining the scenario and seeing the outcome the way you want it to be. An example of a stressful situation is when you are applying for a job. Before going on the interview, imagine you will get the job. Imagine what it will be like to work in this company. Imagine what you'll be doing in your new job and what you would like to make happen in this new position. This will help you be more confident at the job interview and you will be more likely to get the job. What you're doing is conditioning your mind, which causes the rest of you to act confidently in this particular situation. If you imagine yourself not getting the job and imagine you wouldn't know how to handle the job if you got it, you probably won't get it.

Your imagination is powerful

Your imagination is where your creativity begins. Someone imagined lighter than air flying machines before airplanes became a reality, just the way someone imagined computers, palm pilots, digital clocks, credit cards, ballpoint pens, and even pantyhose. All of these things were first ideas in someone's imagination. In the 1940's, most people couldn't imagine a television set in every home. In fact, Daryl F. Zanuck, who was head of the Twentieth Century Fox movie studio said, "Video won't be able to hold onto any market it captures after the first six months. People will soon get tired of staring at a plywood box every night." And he was in the business! Even in the 1960's, few people could imagine a computer in every home. Today, small children tote their laptops to school. Each of these significant changes began in someone's imagination.

When we imagine something, we actually cause it to become reality. It is an idea and then we start to think of it as a possibility. You've seen science fiction movies that had plots that were so far "out there" no one would ever believe they could be real. Yet, within a few years "science fiction" became "science fact" as those scenarios became reality; man orbited the earth and subsequently walked — and even played golf — on the moon.

Use your imagination to change your life

Robin Jay was a very successful advertising account executive. She sold advertising for more than 18 years and consistently exceeded her sales goals. Early in 2001, Robin realized she was unhappy with her work and needed to make a change. She wasn't challenged anymore and had just experienced a close brush with death, which caused her to value each day more than ever. Even though she was successful, she didn't want to waste a single minute of the rest of her life working at a job she didn't like, doing what she didn't want to do, or being where she didn't want to be.

She had always had a vision of herself as a writer and it seemed this was the perfect time to act on her dream. She had heard you are supposed to write about what you know. Since she had been in sales for all those years and had the experience of more than 3,000 client lunches, her friends had nicknamed her, "The Queen of the Business Lunch." She realized she was a Business Relationship Specialist, so she decided to write a book about the art of taking clients out to lunch — what to do, what not to do, and how to make clients feel special. She did an Internet search and was thrilled when she discovered there weren't any books that addressed taking clients to lunch as a means of doing business. Had she discovered a whole new genre? Encouraged by her discovery and eager to beat out anyone else who might be working on such a book, Robin began to spend her Sundays writing *The Art of the Business Lunch*. She even hired an illustrator to create an image of a place-setting with a pen across the plate.

Robin continued to work 50 to 60 hours a week in sales and reserved her weekends for writing. It was challenging to go to work on Monday and listen to others share their stories of their fun or relaxing weekends. She felt tired and unable to recharge her internal batteries. Then 9/11 happened. She discontinued writing, sensing the folly of business lunches in the dawn of a new era of terrorism. By February of 2002, she realized while life in the United States would never be like it was before, business would still continue. Clients still needed to be courted and there was no better way to build a relationship than by sharing a meal. So back to her computer she went.

Due to the demands of her sales job, she was only able to work on the book on Sundays, but she did it because she saw herself as an author. Finally, in the fall of 2003, she attended the Maui Writers Conference. She felt she was on the right track. She returned to work on the book, invigorated and anxious to complete and publish it.

In November of 2003, Robin took a leap of faith and resigned from her sales job. By the end of the year, she had self-published her book. In February of 2004, she hosted a luncheon to announce the launch of her newly published book. During the launch, as she talked about her book, Robin realized how much she enjoyed sharing her stories with others and her presentation was a huge hit; thus a speaking career was born. Robin had found her true calling. She was at home in front of the audience and they related to her and her experiences.

Since the launch of her self-published book, Robin has sold the rights to her book to a well-known publisher. She always said it would happen one day. By 2006, her publisher had already sold the foreign rights to publish her book in five other languages!

I'm giving you the timelines, because I want you to see it took her nearly five years from concept to completion. Things don't always happen as soon as we'd like, but if we are persistent, they will happen.

Robin had a vision, made a plan, worked her plan as well as her other job, gave up a lot of leisure time, allowed for some setbacks, and is finally living the dream she imagined. She gets to stay at home to write and work on programs, do corporate training and convention presentations on her own schedule, and travel across the country giving presentations. Her imagination has certainly served her well. This is exactly the kind of dream that is available to you. Decide what you want to do, believe you can do it, make a plan of how you will do it, and then act on your plan.

You will become as much . . . or as little . . . as you imagine

Marcus Aurelius, Roman philosopher, said, "If the mind of man can conceive an idea and believe it, the man can achieve it." If we can create the image in our minds, we can produce the physical manifestation in our lives, even if such an image has never existed before! When you visualize something, you are establishing new patterns in your brain, the same as if you were actually doing what you are visualizing. You are directing your brain to give you the result you want to achieve. When you plan your day, it works the same way. You are visualizing your day. As you go through your activities, you may have to adjust and modify your actions in order to achieve the result you want by the end of the day.

Is there something you want?

What is your dream? What do you want? Perhaps a new car? Imagine every detail of that car. Will it be a family car or a sports car? Four doors or two? What color would you like? How much horsepower will it have? What will the interior be like? Will the seats be leather or cloth? Visit car dealerships, look at the cars that are for sale, take a demonstration ride, and imagine how you will feel driving that car when you own it.

Perhaps you are looking for a mate? What kind of personality will he have? What values will he have? What interests will he have? How will he treat you?

Maybe you want a great, new job? What would you like to do? What hours do you want to work? Will you wear a uniform or street clothes? What kind of boss will you have, if any?

You will come a lot closer to getting what you want if you know exactly what you want, rather than just having a vague idea or hoping to get something good.

Many people use their imagination in the opposite way. Unsuccessful people are usually unmotivated and unexcited about where they are going. It doesn't really matter what happens; their minds are conjuring up all the things that can go wrong, won't happen, or will disappoint them. *"Oh, I could never own a house like this,"* or *"We won't fit in here."* And guess what! It comes true. They never do own a great house and they don't fit in. They have a general attitude of pessimism which keeps them functioning at a low level of energy. They tend to be more passive and accepting of things as they are, rather than being excited about things as they *can be.*

Don't be like these negative people! Get rid of mental limitations. You can do it simply by imagining and focusing on what it is you ***do*** want, instead of what you ***don't*** want. Whatever you focus on is what you get. So if you focus on what you don't want, you'll get that just as surely as if you focus on what you do want.

Barry told me of an experience in his profession that illustrates this clearly. Barry teaches hang-gliding. In this sport, the hang-glider starts running to the edge of a mountain or hill with a big kite. When she gets to the edge, she pushes out on the triangle-shaped bar that supports the kite, hangs on and soars to the field below. Barry teaches his students to fly toward a particular field where there are acres and acres of openness, and the only obstacle is one small tree in the middle of the field, which should be easy to avoid. Time after time, his students soar right into that tree, sometimes with a mighty impact. Instead of concentrating on where they are going to land, they are focusing on the tree — the one thing they need to avoid.

We all have obstacles around us that we need to avoid. Don't focus on them. Focus instead on where you *do* want to land — whether it is a great new car, a wonderful new job, or a new sense of self worth.

The subconscious part of your mind ignores the words "not" and "don't" and translates the message the same as if you had asked for what you don't want. So if you say, "I am not going to hit the tree," the subconscious hears, "I am going to hit the tree" and directs your conscious mind to do exactly that. Instead, say, "I am landing in the open space," or "I am safely and smoothly gliding to the open field."

Use your imagination creatively

You *can* use your imagination creatively. Create positive pictures in your mind of the things you want to be, do, and have.

Every year for the past 12 years, my business partner, Fiona, and I have created *Goal Achievement Journals* for ourselves on New Year's Eve. These are books we designed in which we write all of our goals for the business and our personal lives for the next year. We write what we want to happen, month by month. We cut pictures, words, and letters out of magazines and paste them into the book. Our goal pages become colorful collages of what it is we desire to achieve and acquire in the coming year.

The first year we did this, we decided on December 28th that we were going to set goals. One of the first goals we identified was to go to Sun City, South Africa and stay in the Palace at the Lost City on New Year's Eve. As it was a new resort and this was the first New Year's Eve the Palace was open for business, rooms were hard to come by and it was only a couple of days away. We called the Palace to make reservations and were told they were completely booked. So Fiona told the reservation person it was very important for us to stay there to set our goals for the New Year, as we were starting a new business and one of our goals for the year was to stay in the Palace. If we could stay at the Palace on the very first weekend of the year, it would prove to us that our other goals could come true as well and give us more enthusiasm to work toward them. The reservationist was sympathetic and said she would see what she could do. About an hour later, we received an invitation to a New Year's Eve party. We didn't want to turn it down . . . unless we could get rooms at the Palace, of course. Fiona called the reservation clerk again and explained she didn't want to be a pest, but she needed to give another person an answer right away. As our goal setting was so important to us, we really needed to know if we were going to get rooms or not. The reservation clerk said she had only one room, and we would have to take it for two nights. Fiona said it would be okay with us to share and reserved the room. The clerk explained it was on the ground floor. That was the best she could do. We thanked her and expressed our appreciation for her efforts on our behalf. When we went to the hotel, we took a small gift for her.

On New Year's Eve day, we arrived at the hotel and Fiona explained to the front desk clerk that we were setting our yearly corporate goals and we really needed to be in a very high place, as we wanted to set very high goals. She asked if there was any way he could give us a great room with a view. He was very gracious and assigned us a huge room on the sixth floor overlooking the elephant walk. You just don't get much better than that. We sent that young man a thank-you gift as well.

Be sure to share your goals with people who can help you get them and ask for their help. People like to help other people, even if they do think you are a bit odd. I'm sure the reservation clerk and the desk clerk thought we were not normal, but they helped us achieve our goal anyway. Be sure to thank people who have helped you. People love to be appreciated.

Daily miracles happen . . . if you believe they will

At the end of every day throughout the year, we record our daily "miracles" in the book. Miracles are the way life responds to our wishes, dreams, desires, and visualizations. In the book, we also write our gratitude for what we have achieved and acquired that day.

You see, what we have done is imprinted our goals in our subconscious minds in colorful pictures. By writing in the book every day, we look at the pictures on a consistent basis. The subconscious mind goes to work making these things happen and making us aware they are happening, so we can take advantage of the opportunities when they are presented to us.

If you are to get what you want, you must first know what you want. The clearer the picture is in your mind, the greater the chance of your achieving of that goal.

Most years, all of our goals have been accomplished by July or August. One year, I pasted a picture of the pyramids in Egypt in my book on the month of May. I actually just pasted it there because I liked the picture. It was an "it would be nice to do" idea, but I didn't have any plans to do it. I didn't think about it again until we got an offer in April to go to Egypt in May to do some work. When we got the offer, my first thought was that I couldn't go because I had too much to do. Then Fiona reminded me I had pasted the picture in the book and caused this to happen in my life. So we went to Egypt, did the training, saw the sights, took a boat trip down the Nile, stayed in a marvelous hotel, and enjoyed fabulous food. And we went first class! Through my creative imagination, I was able to manifest this amazing trip.

There are worlds of possibilities and yet many of us never see them, because we don't think they are possible for us. We think things would be nice to have or do, but then we think negatively; those things aren't for people like us. We have responsibilities.

Pretend you have a fairy godmother and she appears before you this very minute and says she can make all your dreams come true. She insists you be very specific about what you want. Can you be specific?

If you are to have the life you dream of, you must know what you want. In his book, *Psycho-Cybernetics*, the author, Maxwell Maltz, tells us, "A human being always acts and feels and performs in accordance with what he imagines to be true about himself and his environment." It is important for you to imagine being and feeling who and what you want to be. If you are shy, imagine yourself being outgoing and meeting new people with confidence. If you are fearful of a situation, imagine how you would be if you had courage, how you would act, what you would do, and what you would say.

The technique of imagining actually imprints new data into your brain and central nervous system, creating a new self-image. If you will practice "imagining the new you" for a while, you will find you don't need to take any conscious actions, because your subconscious will direct you to act automatically in ways that are consistent with your imagination. This may sound too easy to you . . . almost magical and unbelievable, but I assure you, there is nothing illogical about it. You don't just make a wish and, poof, it happens. It takes conscious effort. As much as we'd like there to be, there's no magic to it. Instead, we have to create a thought which is more powerful than any wave of our imaginary fairy godmother's wand.

Two years ago I wanted a new car, but not just any car. I wanted a Mercedes. They are wonderful cars; well-built, look good, and certainly add status to one's life. They are also expensive and, at the time, a Mercedes was a bit out of my price range, but I decided to practice what I preach. I cut out a picture of the Mercedes I'd like to have and pasted it in my *Goal Achievement* book. Each day as I looked at it, I imagined myself driving that car. In my mind, I could see how good I would look when I picked up my clients at the airport or took them out to lunch or dinner. I imagined how it would feel to have all that luxury. I'd been driving a Volkswagen Beetle for six years and as I am 5'9" tall, sometimes I'd feel more than a little cramped. I daydreamed about how roomy and comfortable a new Mercedes would be. I thought about how nice it would be to have room to stretch my legs. I even imagined how the steering wheel would feel in my hands.

Then one Saturday morning while I was sitting in Spanish class, I heard the man behind me say to another person, "Do you know anyone who wants to buy a Mercedes?" She asked, "Why?" He replied he had bought a Mercedes S430 Lorinzer for his girlfriend and she didn't like driving it. It only had 29,000 miles on it, but she wanted a small Mercedes convertible instead. So, I turned around and jokingly said, "How'd you like a new girlfriend?" Then I told him I would like to look at the car. After class, I took the car for a test drive. It looked and felt exactly like I had imagined. We settled on a price far less than I would have paid at a dealership and everything fell into place just as I imagined it — I had my new car.

Getting the Mercedes is a great example of how creative visualization works. It proves once again that my goal book and my visualization are useful tools. But even though many of our dreams come true, it doesn't mean everything in our lives is all rosy or we don't have challenges. Life doesn't always happen according to our plans. A few months later, my life partner died unexpectedly. This meant I had to find a new place to live. If I had known this was going to happen, I wouldn't have bought the Mercedes. Finances were going to be tight, plus the real estate market in Las Vegas at that time was escalating. Great deals on homes were few and far between. People were paying prices for properties which were inflated beyond true market value and there was a waiting list for both old and new homes. I looked at a lot of possibilities. I even bid on a couple of houses I didn't really want. Of course, I didn't get them. I couldn't visualize myself in them, even though I thought I should get something. I could hear that little voice inside of me saying, "Not for you."

The previous year, I had put a down payment on a small condo I was going to use as a rental property. It was supposed to be finished within a month, so I decided I would move in there and cope with the limited space. But I kept imagining the right place for me was out there somewhere. It came time for me to move from our home and the condo was still not ready. There were numerous mistakes and the construction had been delayed, so some of the rooms were not even completed. The movers were all lined up to move my furniture on Friday and it was now Tuesday. I told the salesman from whom I had purchased the condo that I was not going to move twice and I wanted every penny of my money refunded, including the earnest money. Even though the condo was in escrow, ready to close, he arranged for the return of the entire amount. Then as I started out the door, he said, "Judi, a condo is going to be put on the market tomorrow with the floor plan you originally wanted a year ago when you looked at the models. In fact, it's the very same lot you said would be perfect for you, but it had already been sold. The man who bought it was transferred and he's going to sell it. He's down there now." I walked down the street, knocked on the door, told the man who answered that I had heard he wanted to sell his condo and I would like to look at it. He invited me in. When I walked inside, I knew why the investment condo had not been finished. This one had the exact tile I wanted, was painted in the colors I wanted, had five-inch white baseboards, beautiful light fixtures, wooden blinds … it even had the black granite counters and stainless steel appliances in the kitchen that I had envisioned. The view from the master bedroom had a 180-degree view of the Las Vegas strip, downtown, and the mountains. There were a few things that needed to be repaired, so I told the owner if he could have them finished and ready for me to move in on Friday, I would pay his price. He did! At the time of my offer, I didn't know how I would get the financing by Friday, but I was sure I would find a way. With some creative thinking and a bit of negotiating, it happened. On Saturday morning, I sat on my terrace with a cup of tea wondering why we ever doubt that we will be taken care of. I know God answers my prayers. I had my ideal place to live and my beautiful car. I was starting a new chapter in my life.

Don't settle for things as they seem

You don't have to accept life as it appears to be. You have been given free will in order for you to determine who you want to be and what you want to have and do. Your life is as limitless as your imagination. If you believe it can be done, your mind will start to think up ways to make it happen. In his book, *The Magic of Thinking Big*, David Schwartz states, "Believe, really believe, you can move a mountain and you can. Not many people believe that they can move mountains. So, as a result, not many people do." Well, moving mountains may be just an expression, but I know positively, without a doubt, we can move the obstacles in our lives that seem like mountains.

Think of something you would really like to have or to do. Write it down on a piece of paper. Now make a list of all the reasons why you can have or do this. Every time your mind tells you a reason you can't, put the technique of "opposite thinking" into effect and write down why you can. Don't stop until you have exhausted every possible reason. Many of us defeat our own purpose by telling ourselves what we can't have or do, instead of what and why we can. Next, list all the ways you could possibly get what you want. What options are there?

Feelings of inferiority originate in the imagination

When we imagine we can't learn it or have it, it's too difficult, or we are not smart enough, then the feeling of "not good enough" sets in. If we are told by an influential person in our lives that others are stronger or smarter, we believe the person who told us knows what he or she is talking about and we often don't take the time to find out the reality. We just accept as truth what they say. When we use our imaginations in this negative way, it causes us to lose faith and give away our power. We start to "*should*" ourselves. "I *should* be more like them. I *should* be a better person. I *should* be further along in life at this stage. I *should* have been able to make the relationship work." And along with the *shoulds*, come the "*if onlys*." Now we start to imagine how things would have been *if only* we had been different, *if only* we could be like them, *if only* we could have measured up.

Don't listen when people say, "It can't be done," "It won't work," or "It's impossible." What do they know about your capabilities? Besides, people who tell you why things won't work usually don't know much, aren't willing to explore, and aren't very successful themselves. Always "consider the source" when someone begins to criticize you or dump negativity on your dreams.

Remember the line in the movie, *Field of Dreams*, "If you build it ... they will come?" I know it's true. I've experienced it over and over. In 1968, I imagined owning my own modeling and finishing school. I opened the doors to Universal Models in 1970 and sold it in 1986. In 1980, I imagined myself as a public speaker traveling around the world. So far, my speaking career has taken me to 26 countries on four continents. Over the years, I've imagined owning various cars, items of clothing, and meeting certain people. I put pictures of these in my *Goal Achievement* book and worked toward making the goals happen. Sure enough, they have happened. Last year, I imagined the book you are reading right this minute. The idea starts in your mind, you act on it, and it becomes a reality.

The workshop of the soul

Napoleon Hill, author of *Think and Grow Rich*, said, "The imagination is the workshop of the soul wherein a man's destiny is fashioned." He was right. The imagination is the workshop where our plans are created. You are the owner, the manager, and the supervisor of your workshop. Nothing can go into it, except with your permission. Out of it will come the products you design and manufacture. You produce your products daily: your attitude, your relationships, your financial situation, and your success in life. Your workshop is operating twenty-four hours a day, seven days a week, three-hundred and sixty-five days a year, whether you are aware of it or not. It keeps your entire body functioning. If you want to keep yourself functioning at peak performance, you must program your conscious mind to give the right instructions to the subconscious. When you input thoughts of health, happiness, joy, abundance, and harmony, your imagination will work with you to be the person you want to be and have the life you dream of living.

Charles Kettering, former head of General Motors, once said, "My interest is in the future, because I am going to spend the rest of my life there." That's where you and I are going to spend the rest of our lives as well. We must look forward and imagine a successful future for ourselves.

"But," you say, "I don't know where to begin." It doesn't matter where you begin, as long as you begin. Someone once asked Mother Teresa why she started with only thirty-five cents and she replied, "Because it was all I had." It doesn't matter how much or how little you have, you have to begin somewhere. What matters is where you are going, what purpose you have for living your life, what you are willing to do to make your goals a reality, what you are willing to give up, and what responsibilities you will accept. You must also ascertain who will help you succeed, what decisions you will have to make, whether or not you are prepared to make them, and if you have the discipline to follow through.

Don't look with envy at other people who have created success. You have the same opportunities and abilities as they do. Look at your own life and see how you can rearrange your behavioral patterns to produce the results you want.

In an article entitled, "Creating the Creative Environment" in the *Management Review* of February 1986, Rosebeth Moss Kanter is quoted as saying, "The overall key to creativity is what I call 'kaleidoscope thinking.' The kaleidoscope is a wonderful metaphor for the creative process because the gadget allows us to twist reality into new patterns. In a kaleidoscope, a set of fragments form a pattern, but aren't locked into place. All you have to do is shake it, twist it, change angle, change perspective, and the exact same fragments form an entirely new pattern."

If we want to form new patterns in our lives, then sometimes we have to shake it up a bit, look at things from new angles, and change perspective. In order to do this, we need to make a conscious effort to be aware of what we do and of our environment as well.

Develop the habit of observing what is going on around you. For example, when you see a couple not talking to each other while having dinner in a restaurant, make a mental note of what you see. Observe their body positioning, hand movements, facial expressions, how much eye contact they have and what they are eating. Are they happy in each other's company or are they bored? What are they thinking?

Take time to look at nature. When you see a cloud, notice what kind of cloud it is. How is it shaped? What image does it form? What shade of white is it? Is the cloud moving? Look at the cloud's shadows. What are they covering up?

When you are listening to music on the radio, try to hear each individual instrument. Imagine various people you know playing those instruments or dancing to that music.

Become interested in what's going on around you. Develop your curiosity. It is a key component of kaleidoscope thinking, unlocking your creativity, and forming new patterns in your life.

Einstein once said, "I know quite certainly that I have no special gift except that I have curiosity, obsession, and dogged endurance which, combined with self-critique, have brought me ideas."

Affirm you are creative

Creative people are creative because they believe they are creative. It is important to affirm you are creative in order to anchor the belief in your imagination.

Mark Victor Hansen and Jack Canfield, New York Times best-selling authors of the famous *Chicken Soup for the Soul* books, affirmed ahead of time they would get the perfect title for their book. They repeated the affirmation "mega best-selling title" at least 400 times. They even went so far as to affirm that the perfect title would come to one of them in the middle of the night. According to Mark Victor, "Jack got it. He woke up, got goose bumps and said, 'Chicken Soup for the Soul!' He called me in the middle of the night and we had the title." Today Mark Victor Hansen and Jack Canfield are multi-millionaires. Do affirmations work? It certainly appears they do!

Develop your creative abilities

An inquisitive approach to everything you do stretches your mind. A questioning attitude will help you develop your ability to use your imagination to conceptualize.

When you were a child, you probably drove your parents a bit crazy because you always wanted to know, "Why?"

A UCLA study concluded that children at age five engage in creative tasks 98 times a day, laugh 113 times a day, and ask 85 questions. However, by the age of 44, the numbers shrink to two creative tasks a day, 11 laughs, and six questions.

Further, the UCLA study found a 91 percent negative response rate among adults exposed to new ideas.

Creativity is a fragile and delicate state of mind that is profoundly affected by interactions with others. Stay away from negative people if at all possible.

Exercise your imagination

Imagination is like a muscle and it can be strengthened with exercise the same as physical exercise strengthens your body.

It is imperative you challenge your old assumptions and avoid predictable patterns. Use the "*what if*" technique instead. *What if* we change the angle? *What if* we paint it a different color? *What if* we redesign the main building? *What if* we move our head office to China? *What if* we send Johnny to private school? *What if* we travel to Africa? Let your imagination soar. Change your angle so you view things from new perspectives. Make new connections. Shake things up a bit and take risks. Don't listen when either your inner voice or someone else criticizes your creativity. Lighten up and have some fun.

Use your imagination to create some wonderful adventures. Maybe you no longer imagine yourself as a princess, a cowgirl, or a white rabbit, but there are so many other possibilities waiting for you when you set yourself free from the limitations of other people's expectations, as well as your own. Every day you have the opportunity to use your imagination to create a better life.

———

Imagination Expansion Exercise

You can do this by yourself or with someone you love. Get out an old blanket or a big beach towel, wear some comfortable clothes, and go outside. Find a safe spot to spread out your blanket or towel. Take off your shoes. Now lie down and look up at the clouds. Observe all the shapes and movements of the clouds. Let your imagination show you pictures and faces in the sky.

Then get out your book and write a creative description of one of your dreams. Think of every adjective and declarative statement you can use.

_____

_____

_____

_____

_____

_____

_____

_____

_____

_____

_____

_____

_____

_____

_____

_____

_____

_____

_____

_____

_____

Imagination Affirmation

I play daily in the creative workshop of my soul. I let my imagination run free to build the future of my dreams. I see myself taking all the steps necessary to reach my goals. Mountains move aside and roadblocks melt away as I move resolutely toward success. I bring the joy of my accomplishments into my experiences. I see my success and it is my reality. I am more than enough.

Chapter Five

Talk Yourself Into It

Your internal dialogue powerfully programs and shapes your self-concept. If you believe you are worthy and strong, you will live up to that truth.

— Dr. Phil McGraw, Psychologist and Author

Are people who talk to themselves really crazy? If they are, then we must be, too! We all talk to ourselves. We have a commentary running through our brains about the people and events around us, and how we feel about both. It is often referred to as our internal dialogue. Most of the time, we aren't even aware of it.

In addition, we each have a critic in our head that has its own running commentary about ourselves. Our critic tells us how we feel about situations we are in, and whether or not we are coping with each situation. This critic can destroy us if we allow it to give us "bad" reviews of our performance.

When you talk to yourself

Be sure you always talk to yourself in a positive manner. Your opinion of you is vitally important. We build up or tear down our self-esteem by the thoughts we have. These thoughts create pictures in our minds. These pictures evoke feelings and emotions.

Negative pictures evoke negative feelings and emotions, bringing back every experience where we didn't believe in our capabilities, didn't perform at our best, didn't say something in the right manner, or didn't know how to do something. These pictures remind us of all our hurts and disappointments. Before long they become so vivid, we relive the pain and believe we got what we deserved. Negative self-talk destroys self-esteem.

When you hear that little voice inside your head saying something negative to you, talk back to it. Say, "Thank you for sharing. Now go away." Then say something positive that you know to be true about yourself.

Marcus Aurelius said, "Your life is what your thoughts make it." This is so true! That's why it is mandatory for you to control your thoughts.

Create a mental picture of yourself as a healthy, happy, successful person. Look at all the good features and characteristics you have. Give yourself some positive feedback. Tell yourself all the good things you want and need to hear. What you tell yourself will determine your self image. This is why it's important to talk to yourself with love, kindness, and caring.

Homework assignment

For the rest of your life, you are never again to attach a negative word to the words "I am." Never again are you to say, "I am stupid," "I am dumb," "I am fat," "I am ugly," or anything even remotely similar.

Every statement we make has an effect on our subconscious. Be sure your statements are positive. Attach positive words to the words "I am" such as, "I am a very smart person," "I am creative," "I am at my perfect weight," "I am an attractive person." I call this **Positive, Simple Self-talk** (PSST).

Positive simple, self-talk

PSST . . . you will succeed. PSST . . . use powerful, positive statements that you would like to believe about yourself. Say or write these in first person tense. These are commands you consciously give to your subconscious mind. Some examples are:

★ All things are possible to me if I believe.

★ Every day in every way, my life is getting better and better.

★ All I need is within me now.

★ I am smart. I can find a solution.

★ I have the courage to do whatever it takes.

This positive, simple self-talk, when repeated regularly and continuously, will be accepted by the subconscious part of your mind as reality. The subconscious believes whatever you tell it. In the beginning, it may seem to argue with you a bit. You say, "I'm at my perfect weight." And it says, "No, you're not!" That's because you've been telling yourself that you are overweight for such a long, long time, your mind has come to believe you are overweight. Now you must correct your previous misguided instructions and tell it what you want it to believe. You must tell your subconscious repeatedly and regularly for a period of no less than twenty-one days in order to override the belief system you now have in place.

Your self-concept determines your success

What you believe to be true about yourself is what you make happen in your life. You view the world through your belief system. Since beliefs are usually formed as a result of what someone else told us about our intelligence, our lives, our possibilities, and our circumstances, we've learned to see the world through what we were taught by others. Don't you think it's about time you take charge of your own beliefs? Your self-concept is what determines your performance. You will always take the action that is consistent with your concept of yourself.

Whatever success or lack of success you have in your life is because of what you have believed about yourself up until now. The only way you will change your outcome is to change the way you think. Your thoughts create your feelings. Your feelings direct your behavior. Your behavior brings about your results. You will not have different results in your life until you change your thinking.

With positive, simple self-talk, you can build up your self-esteem, gain courage to do the things you'd like to do, increase your passion for your work and your life, and even take control of your emotions.

You can become everything you want to become, have the kind of people in your life that you would like to associate with, have the things you wish to have, and go the places you dream about as soon as you use your mind in a positive manner and point it in a positive direction.

How badly do you want to succeed? Are you willing to do the work needed? Once you come to terms with the depth of your desires and have clarified your goals, it will be time to take action.

Right now, you must sell yourself on the idea that you can and will make it happen. Reprogram your mind through "auto-suggestion." Tell yourself, "I have the talent, skills, and ability I need to become whatever I choose to be." Repeat this statement a minimum of two times a day for twenty-one days. You will eventually believe it. Write it down and carry it with you. Read it and recite it whenever you can. The more you do this, the more it will become a reality for you. Robert Collier, one of our country's original self-help gurus said, "Any thought that is passed on to the subconscious often enough and convincingly enough is finally accepted."

Write out your positive, simple self-talk statements before you start repeating them. In this way, you can be sure you have the self-talk worded in the best possible way for programming your mind for success.

Self-talk is personal

Self-talk is for your "self." You can't write anyone else's self-talk and they can't write yours. Positive, simple self-talk is used to regulate our own performance. All change starts inside ourselves. We can't change someone else through our thinking. The only person you can change is you. The only person I can change is me. Changing ourselves, and the way we respond to others may ultimately help others feel more comfortable, and this may influence them to act differently in our presence.

Self-talk is positive

Self-talk must be worded in a positive manner. When writing, emphasize gain rather than loss. Don't describe what you don't want. Instead, focus on what you do want. Write the statement so it creates a positive picture in your mind. "I am at my perfect weight of ____ pounds." (Fill in whatever you believe your ideal weight to be.) Phrase it as though you are already there instead of, "I am going to lose 25 pounds." When you say, "I am going to . . ."it puts the action out in the future somewhere. When you make the statement in the present tense, it says "I am there." The subconscious mind starts to work to make your statement true and convert your hope into reality.

The workplace environment

In the average workplace, we hear a minimum of five negative statements every hour. It takes between 14 and 20 positive statements to overcome the effects of one negative statement. Let's do the numbers. If you work a 40-hour week, you hear approximately 800 negative statements a month at work. In addition, some of us live with people who are less than positive, which will raise the numbers even more. It is possible that we are hearing at least 1,000 negative statements every month. If it takes 14 to 20 positive statements to overcome the effects of each negative statement, you need someone to tell you 14,000 to 20,000 good things about yourself every month! You probably couldn't even do that for yourself. This is why it is so important to limit our exposure to negativity.

About 70 percent of the negativity you and I hear every day comes out of our own mouths. We complain about the traffic, the weather, our kids, our spouse, our hair, our body, our clothing, our boss, our teachers, the food in the cafeteria or employee dining room, and a multitude of other things. Take control of what you say. Think before you speak; eliminate negative statements from your dialogue.

Your personal pep rally

Begin and end each day with a private, personal pep rally where you cheer yourself on in order to get a head-start on raising the number of positives for that day. Shortly after awakening, in a very quiet, comfortable place where you won't be disturbed, clear your mind. You can do this by thinking of some place you love to spend time or a restful scene like green hills where you can hear a babbling brook off in the distance. Then think about all the things you have to be grateful for . . . your health, your family, adequate food and shelter, freedom, the right to choose, etc. Remind yourself of the successes you have had in life — big and small, the obstacles you've overcome, and the love you've shared. Think about the strengths and characteristics that make you who you are. Then, tell yourself you will reach your next goal.

Practice this at the beginning of each day and at night before you go to bed. Any time you start to feel depressed or negative, do it again. It's not possible to think two thoughts at the same time, so if you find yourself thinking a negative thought, change it to something positive. Get out your goal book and review your list of accomplishments, strengths, and blessings. This act will push the negativity out of your mind.

Every morning, just after prayer, I do my affirmations. On the days that I am speaking to an audience, my affirmation sounds like this: "I am a powerful and effective speaker. I'm good at what I do. I like people and people like me. Someone in my audience today needs to know what I know. I will remember that information at the right time. I'm powerful. I'm effective. I'm good at what I do. I look good. I smell good. Yeah, me!"

Anchoring

While saying your affirmation aloud, you can anchor your self-talk by physically touching yourself in a place where you can touch yourself again in public. I anchor my positive self-talk by pressing on the palm of my left hand with the thumb of my right hand while I am saying the affirmation. Our bodies have memory and if I get aggravated during the day, I put my hands together and push my thumb into the palm of my other hand. It's like turning the switch of a tape recorder to the "on" position. My subconscious mind replays the affirmation. It starts to tell me, "I am powerful and effective." I've been doing this for many years now and it has served me well.

There was one occasion when I had just started my day and I asked the audience, "What are your goals for the program? What do you want to get out of today?" I do this in order to find out what they want to learn during the time we are together. As they tell me their goals and objectives, I list them on a flip chart. On this particular day, as I turned to write on the chart, a voice in the back of the room said, "Well, if you don't know, I guess nobody does." So I turned around and said, "Excuse me?"

The voice from the back said in a louder, nastier tone, "If you don't know what we are here for, you shouldn't be here. After all, you're the trainer who put out a brochure that lists point by point what we are supposed to learn. Maybe you should have read it." I pressed my thumb hard into the palm of my other hand, looked to see if I could read his name tag, and said, "Tony, is it?"

"Yeah, it's Tony," he replied.

I said, "Tony, I'm a bit confused . . ."

Before I got the opportunity to finish the sentence, he said, "It's pretty @#!%#! obvious you are confused. It's pretty @#!%#! obvious you are stupid. It's pretty @#!%#! obvious we are in for another wasted day with another stupid, woman trainer."

"Oh, no, Tony," I said. "I'm not confused about the material. I'm confused about us. What's happening here with us?"

He said, "There ain't no us and there ain't gonna be, so don't get your hopes up."

I was pressing my right thumb harder and harder into my left hand as I continued, "Have we met? Did I register you this morning?"

"No," he said. "We haven't met."

"Then, if I understand you correctly, it's not me who has offended you? What exactly *is* the problem?"

More quietly, he replied, "It's the last woman trainer we had. She started out the same way as you and she was soooooo stupid."

As he said that, the rest of the group started yelling, "Yeah."

Now I was looking at a few hundred nasty people, instead of just one. I was pushing my thumb into my hand so hard that I thought it would come out the other side. So I said, "Tony, here's what I can do. If you aren't happy by noon today, I'll give your money back for the entire conference. Will that make you happy?"

At that point, the others calmed down, because they figured if I'd give Tony's money back, I'd give theirs back as well. He replied, "It won't make me happy, but it's a deal." So I thought we were okay and I turned to continue writing on the board. As I turned, he said, "But you'd better be @#!%#! good!" I turned back to face him and said, "I am good. I'm one of the best trainers in America today. You stay with me and you'll be happy."

He replied even more nastily, "Well then, get on with it." And I did.

I didn't know if I was one of the best trainers in America. I hadn't even been in America for the past eight years, but I knew I had to show strength or he'd bury me right then and there. If this had happened to me before I learned my anchoring technique, I'd have probably cried, run from the room, and never spoken in public again. Or maybe I would have picked up the nearest book and thrown it at him. Either action would have been ineffective and unacceptable.

By anchoring my self-esteem in place, Tony's words didn't upset me. He wasn't angry with me. He was upset about a previous situation. Because I handled the situation well, the audience had more faith in me. The morning training went well, even though Tony sat there with his arms crossed and an unpleasant facial expression. Right before we broke for lunch, I said, "I'm going to go over the objectives now to see if we are on track with accomplishing our goals for the day. Tony, if this will upset you in any way, please go ahead and wait in the hallway while I review. I will be there in a moment to arrange for your refund."

He stood up and said, "Some days I can be a real @!#*!. This morning I was being a big one. I owe an apology to everyone in this room. Most of all Judi, I owe an apology to you and you can go to lunch with me if you want to."

"No, thank you, Tony. I have other plans for lunch." My plan was to get as far away from him as I could for that hour, so I could renew my energy.

When your self-esteem is anchored, you can focus on your goals and on what the other person is saying between the lines instead of taking the attack personally. My goals as a trainer are always to create a learning environment, share information, transfer the learning, and make a difference in the audience's lives in whatever way I can.

Quiet the negative voice

When you focus on your goals, you are concentrating on what you want to achieve, rather than on what can go wrong or what might happen. You simply can't think two thoughts at the same time. You can go from one to the other. You can even do it quickly, but you can't hold two opposing thoughts in your mind at once. It's impossible. So take control of your mind. When you start thinking anything negative and your little voice starts creating doubt or fear, speak back to it. Use your "Thank you for sharing. Now go away." statements. Then make a new, positive statement to yourself. You can change any picture in your mind by focusing on what you want your mind to see.

What is your little voice saying when things haven't gone as you thought they should? Are you hearing statements like:

- ★ Things never work out for me.

- ★ I can't ever make anything work.

- ★ I'll never be out of debt.

- ★ I should have done it differently.

- ★ I must be stupid. No one ever listens to me.

- ★ I could have done better than I did.

- ★ I really made a fool of myself.

- ★ It's just no use.

- ★ I didn't have the advantages they did.

- ★ It's impossible for me.

Get rid of this negative self-talk. It causes you to sabotage yourself.

Changing from negative to positive

Try this interesting exercise. Think of what you had for lunch. Next, think of a pink elephant. Now try to think of them both at one time. Don't tell me the elephant was eating your lunch! Did you just get a picture of that? When you hear it, your mind sees it. It doesn't matter if I said "don't" or "not to," your mind sees it anyway.

If we can't think of two thoughts at one time, we can't be negative and positive at the same time. Like many people, it's possible you have a habit of allowing yourself to think negatively. Once the habit is there, it's not easily changed. If you want to be a positive thinker, you can be, but it will take work. Good results usually take discipline. You can do it.

Success is not an accident

Successful people make themselves successful. They have goals, dreams, desires, wants, and needs. They develop an attitude that attracts success.

When people ask them how they are, they say, "Wonderful," "Marvelous," or "Terrific." They show interest in other people by replying, "And you; how are you?" They show genuine interest in the other person by listening to that person's answer and commenting afterwards in a positive way. When you ask negative people how they are, they say things like, "Oh, better than nothing," or "Not so good." Sometimes they even go into long, drawn-out dissertations on all their problems. The most positive words that come out of their mouths are, "Not bad," "Alright," or "Okay." These are almost always spoken in a tone that lets you know things really aren't okay at all.

When someone asks you about another person, say something positive about that person. If you don't know anything positive, keep your comments to yourself. Whenever you say bad things about another person, it reflects poorly on you — even more than it does on the person you are talking about. It also identifies you as a gossip.

There's an old saying, "Little people talk about other people. Average people talk about things. Great people talk about ideas and possibilities." Which of these people do you want to be?

Pay compliments to people

If you see someone doing something well, looking good, or being kind to someone else, compliment him or her. When people are rewarded for their behavior they will repeat that behavior. Remember, too, when you say something positive to someone else, you hear it as well. You are raising your own positive statement ratio. It only takes a few seconds to say, "You do your job very well," "You look very good in that color," or "How nice of you to help that man with his packages." You'll be amazed at how good you feel after you pay a compliment to someone else. Many people have told me they don't have time to compliment others, or they are afraid the other person may think they are strange or forward. If that's true, why is it they have time to find fault with others and complain about them? Why would you care if someone thinks you are strange, especially if you are strange in a good way?

Make someone's day

Many years ago, Fiona, my business partner, told me about a technique for giving compliments called the "Five Penny Technique." Here's how it works. Put five pennies in your right-hand pocket every morning and during the day pay compliments to five different people. Each time you pay a compliment, you move a penny to your left-hand pocket. Compliments must be honest and sincere. You can't say something just to move a penny. You can't go home at night until you have moved all five pennies to the left pocket. In the beginning, it was difficult for me to make myself do this. In fact, there were a few nights when I had to stop at a service station or the pharmacy on my way home to find some people to compliment, so that I could move the last of my pennies and go home. People were so thrilled to be complimented that I made a rule for myself. "Whenever I think something good about someone and I'm in a position to say it, I must say it." Obviously, I can't stop in the middle of a speech or a training class and say, "You have great hair," or "The color of your eyes is stunning." But I can compliment people on their participation and their thoughts or ideas. At the break, I can pay a more personal compliment in a tactful way.

One day I was conducting a training class in a conference room at a large hotel. I was staying overnight in the same hotel. After class, I took the elevator back to the floor where my room was located and a very good-looking young man got on the elevator. He was dressed like he was going to model for the cover of *GQ* magazine. I thought to myself, "WOW!" Then I had a series of thoughts that went like this:

"I should tell him how good he looks."

"No, you're an older woman and he'll think you are hitting on him."

"Well, so what? Tell him."

"No." "Yes." "No." "Yes." "No."

"Yes. The floors are going by and if you don't tell him soon, he'll be gone and you will have missed your opportunity."

So I said, "Excuse me. I need to tell you something."

He said, 'Yes ma'am, what is it?"

I said, "You are the most gorgeous man I have seen in a long, long time. You really know how to dress."

He said, "Do I know you?"

I said, "No. Would you like to?" At this point, he started pushing the elevator buttons really fast. He wanted out of that elevator. I don't know about him, but it sure made my day. Even now, when I think of it, I smile all over again.

My friend, Greg, paid a compliment to a clerk in a department store recently. She started to cry and said, "You don't know how much I needed that today. No one has said anything nice to me in a long time."

We never know when saying something positive might "make someone's day." Sometimes the people who look the most put-together need a compliment more than others. It's always a good idea to say something positive to someone. We all need to feel appreciated.

Giving instructions

When you need to give instructions or outline a plan of action to someone else, word your requests or instructions in a positive way. Instead of saying, "I know you aren't going to like this, but the boss wants us to double our sales this month," say, "We've got a real opportunity here. The boss wants us to double our sales this month." Instead of saying, "We are going to have to make some changes around here," say, "Here's some good news. We're going to be making some positive changes." If you want other people to be excited, you have to be excited first. If you want other people to be positive, you must be positive first.

Excitement breeds support. It's contagious. Others will feel your energy, believe in you, and want to be around you. Many will want to help you become even more successful.

PSST . . . make it a habit

PSST . . . Through your self-talk, you exert control over your life. Do this all day, every day. Successful people make a habit of using positive, simple self-talk to influence themselves. When they are feeling good about themselves, they are more able to give compliments and influence others. Think about the habits you have now. How many of them came about by a conscious plan and how many of them did you acquire accidentally or because of outside influences? Many of us learn our habits from the people with whom we spend a lot of time. If we were told by parents, teachers, or siblings that we were clumsy, ugly, stupid, a big ox, or just no good, it's very possible we started to believe whatever they said and even began to repeat it to ourselves. One of my sisters told me how clumsy I was over and over as I was growing up. So I went to modeling school to learn how to walk gracefully. Yet even today, if I trip or stumble, I can still hear her voice in my head saying, "See, I told you that you are clumsy." I talk back to her voice by saying, "This could have happened to anyone. I'm actually very graceful most of the time." Once when I was speaking to a big audience, I walked too close to the edge of the stage, lost my balance and fell off! I heard the audience gasp when I fell. Luckily, I landed on my feet and wasn't hurt, so I ran back up on the stage and said to the audience, "Can you believe I once owned a modeling school and taught hundreds of people how to walk?" We all got a good laugh out of that. I'm sure they were all wondering, "What would I have done if that had happened to me?"

At one time in my life, if I'd fallen off the stage, I would have been so embarrassed I might never have walked onto another stage again as long as I lived. Now, I remind myself I'm human. Falling off a stage could happen to anyone. The important thing is getting back up.

Deliberate conscious control

Learn to take *deliberate, conscious control* of your self-talk and your actions. Write down one bad habit you have — maybe it's telling yourself you're stupid or maybe you gossip about others. Write out what you will do to stop this behavior. That's right. You must consciously decide to do or say something else instead. We don't give up bad habits; we replace the negative action with a positive one. If you hear your little voice talking negatively inside your head, tell it to "Stop" and then replace that thought with something positive. We are all human. We all make mistakes. We all fall down occasionally. We must pick ourselves back up, talk as kindly to ourselves as we would to someone else in the same circumstances, and then go on.

When we deliberately and consciously cultivate the habit of talking to ourselves in a positive manner, we are taking major steps toward everything we desire — successful relationships, financial freedom, material possessions, happiness, and confidence within. We'd be crazy not to talk to ourselves!

PSST . . . Self-talk Exercise

Start by writing out what you want to believe about yourself. Follow these steps:

1. Identify the concern or concerns you want to deal with and then identify the results you want. Write them down. Your concern might be a lack of confidence. The result you want might be to feel confident, courageous, and strong.

2. Write positive statements for each of your concerns expressed as though it is already a reality. For example, if lack of confidence is a concern, instead of writing, "I am nervous," or "I am afraid," write "I am a confident person."

3. Repeat your statements aloud each day for a minimum of 21 days. If your mind resists or argues, tell it to "Stop," or "Thank you for sharing." Repeat your affirming statements again.

4. Write your statements on 3" x 5" cards. Carry one with you. Place some of them where you will see them often, such as your bathroom mirror, the refrigerator door, the visor in your car, or next to your telephone. Continue practicing until your mind has accepted these statements as true and you have achieved your desired result.

1. _____

_____

_____

2. _____

_____

_____

3. _____

4. _____

_____

_____

5. _____

_____

_____

6. _____

_____

_____

7. _____

_____

_____

Self-talk Affirmation

I am free of limitation and negativity. My life is filled with endless possibilities. I face each new challenge with energy and enthusiasm, knowing that I am capable of creating my own success. I am more than enough.

Chapter Six

Believe You Can

Every individual human being born on this earth has the capacity to become a unique and special person, unlike any who has ever existed before or will ever exist again.

— ELIZABETH KÜBLER-ROSS
AMERICAN PSYCHIATRIST AND WRITER

This is an age of specialization. The more information available, the more important it becomes for us to have specialized knowledge. No one can know everything about everything. Learn a lot about a little and get a broad overview of the rest. In other words, become an expert in a particular area.

Recognize your strengths

There are numerous ways you can assess your strengths. You can make a list for yourself or you can ask people you know to help you list your strengths. You can take an assessment like the Myers-Briggs or the SELF-communication style profile. You might want to pick up a copy of Richard Nelson Bolles' book on assessment, *What Color is Your Parachute?* It may be advantageous to hire a professional counselor or coach who can help you determine your strengths and can possibly advise you on taking the shortest and straightest route to your goal.

Imagine yourself succeeding

The more you can imagine yourself accomplishing what you dream about, the more likely you will be to get it. If you can't see yourself succeeding, you will most likely **not** recognize an opportunity when it presents itself. You may even sabotage yourself or turn it down when it's offered to you.

Enlist support

Let family and friends know what it is you want. Family members who love us and good close friends will support us in our quest. They don't always have the knowledge and expertise to guide us, but they can usually make suggestions. We never know when one of those suggestions will be the one we need.

When you are trying to sell someone else on your ideas or your goals, do it enthusiastically. No one will get excited unless you are excited. When I was about 20 years old, I worked for an entertainment company that represented some of the top entertainers at the time. The owner of the company was a well-known, very successful songwriter who had discovered and developed the careers of many young singing groups into top performers and celebrities. It was my job to create the fan clubs and do the publicity and promotions for these groups. Part of this job was interviewing and hiring screamers. Yep, that's what I said, "Screamers." A screamer is a person who is hired to be at the location where you are going to bring the entertainer. When the entertainer gets out of the limo, the screamer jumps up and down, acting really excited, and screams out, "Oh look. Look who's here!" and yells out the name of the group or the entertainer. I learned quickly if you can get two or three good screamers, you can get a crowd to form to see who is getting out of that limo. Before long, everyone is screaming and excited. When there are enough screamers, the new entertainers become stars.

I started thinking about this and began to wonder how average people who work at average jobs get screamers. The answer: We need to do what we do so well people want to come and do it with us. Do it so well they'll even want to bring other people along so they can do it, too.

We all need screamers to support us, help generate excitement around us, and announce our success. Build your cheering section by being excited about what you are doing and deliberately associate with people who are genuinely interested and excited with you. Let them know what you have accomplished so far, so they can applaud and cheer for you. Each cheer will give you a boost and help raise you to the next level of success and more cheers!

You may not believe you need to hear the screamers, but you will be surprised how good it makes you feel when you do. Every day that I have a presentation to give, my business partner leaves me a voice message to encourage me for the day. I'll pick up my messages and hear, "Good luck, Jude. Knock 'em alive today! You are a fabulous speaker. You are worth more than they can ever pay you." These words of encouragement let me know that someone cares whether I succeed or not, and that someone is there for me. I do the same for her. It makes a difference knowing you have a screamer or two in your corner.

Dare to be passionate

Passion is an integral part of achieving success. People with passion have a sense of purpose and meaning. They are achieving things. They don't waste their time. If you feel strongly enough about something, you will put your effort and time toward it. You will be passionate and you will make your dreams come to life. If you don't feel strongly about something, it won't matter to you if it ever gets done or if anything changes.

Malcolm Forbes, publisher of *Forbes Magazine*, is quoted as saying, "Your adrenaline has to run. If you don't feel exhilarated by achieving your objectives and excelling at what you are doing, then you'll never do much very well." Do you know what makes your adrenaline run?

Dare to be passionate about your relationships, your values, your beliefs, and your job. Passion is like a magnet. It attracts the things and people we want in our lives. Passion energizes us and helps us overcome fear. When we are passionate, we experience higher levels of joy, love, and satisfaction.

Passionate people make things happen

Florence McClure was not a public speaker. She was a hotel executive. Florence became so outraged by the lack of resources and respect for victims of sexual assault in our community that she started speaking out. Her passion for eliminating the abuse of women and children led her not only to speaking at club and organization luncheons, but to lobbying at local, state, and federal levels. As a result, she overcame any fear she had of public speaking. She returned to college and earned a bachelor's degree in sociology. In 1973, she and Sandi Petta co-founded Community Action Against Rape. Under her leadership, CAAR was able to change the way law enforcement treated victims of rape. Hospitals began to keep rape kits on hand and police attended sensitivity training.

Through her constant efforts to improve the lives of women, Florence soon became known as "Hurricane Flo," because when she got passionate about something, watch out! Nothing stood in her way. She could knock down big obstacles with a single passionate speech. She could get the tightest misers to open their wallets. Think about this. It was 1973 and she was a woman speaking out about a subject that, at that time, didn't concern many men or even some women. She went on to champion the cause of Nevada's incarcerated women and even got the state to locate the women's prison near Clark County, so the prisoners could be closer to their children. Her passion not only overrode her fear, it also changed the lives of thousands of women for the better.

What could your passion do if only you would unleash it? Passion is like the wind in our sails. It pushes us in the direction we want to go. Without passion, we might never leave the harbor. If we allow our passion to die, we might end up on the rocks or stuck in the doldrums of mediocrity.

How do you find your passion?

Passion comes when we believe in something, when our purpose is clear. Passion is the fuel that drives us to accomplish our goals. If your tank is full of passion, you are going to go a long way.

What gets you excited? What do you love? What do you feel strongly about in your life? What would you do even if you didn't get paid? What are your special talents? How do you know when something is right? Have you tried to do something that you've never done before? What do you secretly wish you could do? How badly do you want to do it?

Listen to your heart

Listen to your heart to find what it is you want to do and what you feel passionate about. Then you can put your entire focus into it, rather than just getting up, getting dressed, going to work, and getting through the day. When you are excited about life, you'll get up early, be on time, do your best, give more than is expected, and be happy doing it. If you don't feel this, perhaps you need to make some changes. If your job isn't as satisfying as you would like, maybe you need a new job. Perhaps it won't pay as much or won't have the perks your current job has, but when you condition your mind, it will change the condition of your life. The money will come when you love what you do and have enthusiasm for it.

If you are willing to accept a job you don't like, one that creates stress, but pays well, then you have to be willing to pay the price, and the price you pay is a lack of passion and joy. Many of us have been taught from childhood that it is selfish and self-centered to be happy in what we do. We've been taught we must work hard to get ahead. If we can learn to work passionately, we will go further than hard work will ever take us.

Samantha had a very demanding job that paid her $125,000 a year. She worked long, stressful hours six, and sometimes seven, days a week. In addition, her boss often needed her to attend social events. Her job consumed her life. After a couple of years, she lost her love for the job. Eventually, she began to hate it, but she didn't know where else she could make the kind of money she was making with her limited education. Samantha told me her hate of that job became her passion. It was a negative passion. She said, "I worked long and hard hours. I met all my department objectives and then some. I felt unappreciated and I knew I didn't get the recognition I deserved. I pushed everyone who reported to me to be better and better. I became critical, overbearing, and driven to be right. I felt stuck and I was going to make the best of it. And here's the kicker; I was fired! I didn't leave that job willingly. I had to be thrown out."

Then she added, "Now that I have some distance from it and I can think clearly, I realize I was fired because I had become unhappy, negative, and inefficient in my job. I have a new job now that I love. I'm happier, healthier, and even though I am making a lot less money, the quality of my life is better. I am now using my talents and skills daily. There are a lot of opportunities with this new company, as long as I keep my life in balance and my attitude in check. It's been a long road back."

If you keep doing the same old thing in the same old way . . . only harder and longer, you are going to get the same old results and you are going to hate it. Life treats you as you treat life. In order to be passionate about life, you may have to undergo a mind change. You may need to re-evaluate what's really important to you. As you observe your life and the lives of others, you might see that living a life without passion is a costly compromise. It is much easier to live a life of passion than it is to live a stressful, unhealthy, unfulfilling, though well-paid existence.

When we have passion, our minds let go of blocks and barriers, because we are focused on what we wish to accomplish and the expectation of what good we can make happen. When we are passionate, we take great joy in our steps forward — both big and small, using what didn't work as lessons learned, setting new goals, and moving onward and upward to achieve these new goals. In other words, when we are passionate, we just get on with it!

Be enthusiastic

The word enthusiasm comes from the Greek words, *en theos*, which mean "the spirit within." We each need to unleash the spirit that is within us. You can't expect other people to get excited about your ideas or projects if you aren't excited. If you don't have a tone of enthusiasm in your voice, people won't buy into your ideas. If you can focus your enthusiasm toward achieving your goal, others will want to help you achieve it.

My first business

When I started my first business, I had a total of $2,000 in my savings account. I found a small office to rent, paid a security deposit, and my first and last month's rent. After buying my office furniture and the supplies I needed to run my business, I didn't have any money left, but I was determined to be successful. The first day of the second month came and the rent was due. I contacted my landlord, Mr. Ray Paglia, and told him I didn't have the money to pay the rent. I asked him to allow me credit for a month. Mr. Paglia looked at me and said, "The man in the business next door bet me you wouldn't last in business six months. I bet him you would. If you can hang in there for six months, I'll make enough money on the bet to cover your rent. Do you think you can hang in there?" Because of his belief in me, I was able to "hang in there" those six months.

I was so enthusiastic about my goal. I believed in my dream enough to go after it and to ask for credit when I needed it. Mr. Paglia believed in me enough to give his support. This gave me even more confidence to believe in myself. After that rough start, I became quite successful. For the next 17 years, I ran an extremely well known and profitable modeling school, agency, and convention-service business. I even received a Las Vegas Chamber of Commerce "Woman of Achievement" Award!

Walter Chrysler, the American automobile pioneer, said, "The real secret of success is enthusiasm. You can do anything if you have enthusiasm. Enthusiasm is the yeast that makes your hope rise to the stars. Enthusiasm is the sparkle in your eye. It is the swing in your gait, the grip of your hand, the irresistible surge of your will, and the energy to execute your ideas. Enthusiasts are fighters. They have fortitude. They have staying qualities. Enthusiasm is at the bottom of all progress. With it, there is accomplishment. Without it, there are only alibis."

Expose yourself to new opportunities

When I owned Universal Models, there was a talented South African photographer, Vimmi, who was living in Las Vegas. The agency did a lot of work with him. He would often stop by my office and jokingly say, "Come to South Africa with me." I like a good joke, so I instructed my secretary to buy a plane ticket to South Africa. "Make sure I have the seat next to his. We'll tell him I'm going to South Africa with him and then we'll cash in the ticket."

When I showed him the plane ticket, he was beyond surprised. He was shocked. You should have seen his face! He said he often invited people to go with him, but no one had ever taken him up on it before. I thought it was so funny. However, when I asked the airline for a refund, it wasn't so funny. My ticket was non-refundable. I guess the secretary didn't hear the part about getting my money back. The joke was on me. I was stuck with the ticket.

Since I had only been out of the United States once, and that was barely over the border into Mexico, I decided I might as well go. I set out on the adventure of my life with a person I hardly knew. I was scared. Once we got on the plane, he said to me, "Don't expect me to entertain you. I'm going home to see my family and friends and not to do tourist things." Then he took a sleeping pill, went to sleep, and didn't talk to me again until we landed in Johannesburg. That comment didn't make me any more confident or comfortable.

Vimmi's mother picked us up at the airport and drove us downtown to the Landrost Hotel, where they left me. After they were gone, I realized that I was all alone in a country which I had never been to before and didn't know much about. After checking into my room, I went to the concierge and explained my predicament. He was delighted to book me on a different tour every day. It was too late for a tour that day, so the concierge advised me to walk around the city, not to carry a purse, and to tuck in my shoe whatever money I took with me. He also advised me to put my camera in a paper bag, so I wouldn't look like a tourist. I did as instructed. I walked around downtown and also visited model agencies and introduced myself. I quickly made some friends and had a great time.

A couple of days later, Vimmi called to tell me he was felt guilty about leaving me at the hotel, and was coming to take me to Sun City to see the Julio Iglesias show. He picked me up with his mother, Marti, who had been one of South Africa's top models. We not only went to see Julio's show, we met Julio and spent time talking with him at the pool on a couple of occasions.

In addition to meeting Julio, they made sure there were many other highlights in my trip, including spending time in the Kruger National Park, where I saw wild animals up close and personal. We went sight-seeing in Cape Town, had dinner with South Africa's top fashion designer, and spent several days on the beach.

There are several points to this story:

★ I hadn't taken a vacation in years and was on the verge of burn-out. By putting some distance between me, and my everyday life, I came back refreshed, rested and with new energy.

★ The touring I did by myself gave me a new confidence, as I talked with people I might not have if I had been accompanied.

★ Experiencing new cultures, seeing things I had never seen, and doing things I had never done caused me to look at my life differently.

★ Meeting and visiting people in another country who were in the same business as me enabled me to network and share ideas and business practices.

★ We never know where a new experience will take us, or who we will have the opportunity to meet. This experience caused me to fall in love with South Africa. When the opportunity presented itself six years later to live and work in Johannesburg, I jumped at the chance. I had found my passion . . . Africa.

Make the choice to be happy

How can we be happy and passionate every day when we are dealing with the stresses of life? Your world is what you make it, through your thoughts, words, and attitudes. Focus on the positives. Stop worrying. Do what the title of Richard Carlson's book says, *Don't Sweat the Small Stuff . . . and It's All Small Stuff.* Worrying doesn't accomplish anything. Worrying simply strangles our creative abilities and keeps us from being able to look for solutions to our problems and challenges. Your brain knows how to think and if allowed, it will create the right things to do and say. Most of us don't take time to think. We don't spend time alone in the quiet. If we are alone, we usually have the television or the radio blaring, forcing our brain to work at taking in information rather than doing what it needs to do. Research tells us the average American household has the television on at least seven hours a day. Each year, television programming becomes increasingly more violent, inane, and abusive. The negative energy it puts into our lives becomes more difficult to overcome. We are subconsciously programming ourselves to be negative by what we are watching. We learn to accept the abuse and the violence in our world. We come to believe it is the norm. We are numb to it, even hypnotized by it. If we hear our friends talking about a program we haven't seen, we feel left out. So we start watching whatever violent or ridiculous show is the rage and we become addicted to it — drawn into the story line and programmed subconsciously to watch it. We don't do this because we like the show, but simply to find out what happened. We turn that radio or television on the minute we wake up or walk into the house, because we don't know how to be alone with our thoughts. We don't know how to listen to our inner voice. We may even be afraid of what we will hear.

We are never inactive in our thought. We are either going forward or going backward. Most people don't understand this. They reach a certain point in life and they stop making any effort to learn, develop, or progress. It's important for you to realize you can always go further. As Napoleon Hill said, "If you can conceive it and believe it, you can achieve it." When you expand your thoughts, you will do and have greater things.

Turn off the television and the radio for at least 20 minutes a day and spend that time in silence by yourself. Put positive thoughts in your head. Your subconscious doesn't care what you put into it. It will respond to any thought it receives. Focus on your biggest goal and mentally see yourself achieving it or having it. This will prove to you that life has very few limits for you. When you program your mind with positive thoughts, you realign your body chemistry and make yourself healthier and happier. When you think and behave in a positive manner, you not only cause others to enjoy the experience of being around you, you keep yourself energetic and make your life more exciting.

Happy in spite of the circumstances

When I lived in South Africa, I often wondered how people could come to work so clean and happy without having indoor plumbing, running water, heat, air conditioning, flooring, or windows in their little shacks made of tin, cardboard, and black plastic trash bags. I knew many of them had to walk miles and often stand out in bad weather for long periods of time to catch a taxi. The taxis were actually vans designed to seat nine people, but 16 would cram into them. Many people had to transfer taxis more than once, and sometimes were dropped off at points that still left them with miles to walk to get to their places of work. Yet, they would come through the door with smiles on their faces and I could often hear them singing as they worked. When I asked one of the African women with whom I worked why she was so happy, she told me it was because she could "feel within herself a unity with the Spirit of God." She further stated, "God makes all things right. God shows me the best out of my experiences, forever guides me, and provides me with my daily needs. God gives me the will to go on, the determination to be the best I can, and the joy of becoming more every day." This was before the end of apartheid, and yet here was an African woman who had made up her mind to be happy in spite of all the prejudices against her and the restrictions put on her life by the government — for no other reason than the color of her skin.

Happiness lies within us

Nice homes, clothes, cars, or other material things can make our lives easier and more comfortable, but they don't necessarily make us happy. We've all known people who have almost everything money can buy and still they are miserable. Happiness is in our hearts and our minds. Happiness is a way of looking at life. It is first a decision and then it becomes a habit.

Tell your face

While attending a seminar to observe another presenter, I noticed a woman sitting in the third row with her arms folded tightly across her chest and a terrible scowl on her face. She sat like that all morning. At the break the presenter, Carol, went over to the woman and said to her, "Did you come to get anything in particular today?" The woman didn't change her body language or her facial expression one bit and curtly said, "I'm fine." So Carol continued, "Well, if there is anything you think of that you might like me to cover, just let me know." The woman again said, "I'm fine." This went on with Carol trying to get the woman to be a bit more pleasant and the woman continuing with her curt, "I'm fine," answer. Then I heard Carol say, "Well then, why don't you tell your face?" The woman burst out laughing.

After the seminar, I confronted Carol, "You are so lucky that woman laughed. How could you say something like that to someone in your audience? She is your customer." Carol replied, "I don't know. It started in my feet and it just worked its way up my body. Before I knew it, it was out of my mouth. I don't have a rewind button. I couldn't take it back."

Later, when I was thinking about this, it dawned on me how often many of us forget to *"tell our faces"* we are okay. We get so caught up in our daily chores and challenges that we may speak to someone or answer a question without adjusting our faces. We need to be more aware of what our faces are telling others and change our body posture, demeanor, and cial expression to look like that of a happy person. It's called "acting as if" or "fake it until you make it." The very act of changing to a more positive outward expression will make us feel better inwardly.

Look on the bright side

The subconscious part of our minds is the place where our memories are stored. Our present happiness is influenced by those memories. If we do things today that make us feel happy, content, peaceful, or joyful, this will increase our happy memories. The more happy days we have, the more happy memories we create. The more happy memories we have, the more happy days we create. What goes around comes around. It's the happiness cycle and the more you do it, the easier it gets.

As children, most of us were told by an adult at one time or another that we should "look on the bright side." Sometimes it's not easy to do. Some situations don't seem to have a bright side. In most situations, there is at least something good we can learn from it. We might have to look for it, but it is there. Most successful people believe "everything happens for a reason." Looking on the "bright side" simply means to look for what's right, what you can learn, and realize things could be worse. We can learn a lesson from the goldfish swimming in a fish bowl half-filled with water. One fish said to the other, "Is this bowl half-full or half empty?" The other fish said, "I don't really care. I'm just glad it's enough." Are you glad you are enough? Or are you looking at your life as though it's half-full or half-empty?

Stop for a minute and think about the times in your life when you were the happiest. I'm not talking about events such as receiving an award, getting married, graduating, or even getting a divorce where you exclaimed, "This is the happiest moment of my life." I'm talking about expanded periods of time in your life when you felt content, joyful, cheerful, or even blissful. Wasn't it when you were doing one of the following?

★ Participating purposefully in life

When you act purposefully, you are putting faith into action, going after your goals or doing something that makes life better for yourself or others. When you put your faith into action, you are giving up uncertainty, doubt, and fear. When I started Universal Models with only $2,000,

I knew in my heart that I would have a successful business. I was going after my goals and my dream. Uncertainty, doubt, and fear never entered my mind. I knew the city of Las Vegas needed a legitimate model agency and I was positive I could make that happen. I knew conventions needed dependable personnel who could work in the exhibits as sales people, hostesses, receptionists and spokespersons. I knew that movies filmed in Las Vegas would need "extras." I knew beauty pageants needed to be run in a legitimate manner, assuring that the contestant with the most points was the one who became the contest winner. Most of all, I knew I could organize all of this and make it happen. I knew models, actors, and other part-time personnel needed to be paid as soon as possible after completing their work. I did it all and I was happy. I loved my business and the people with whom I dealt.

★   Being creative

Creativity requires playfulness, fun, humor, daydreaming, and letting go of negative programming. Boisterous laughter is energy producing and can have the same beneficial effect as running. Laughter and humor are also beneficial for adjusting and reducing major life stresses. When we increase our energy, reduce our stress, and use our natural instincts, we free ourselves from limited thinking which allows us to see the bright side.

My friend, Jill, graduated from college owing large balances on her student loans. She brainstormed all of the legal ways she could make a lot of money fast. Since she had just gotten a great education, she decided to use it. She auditioned to be on game shows. She became a contestant on three game shows the following year and won a total of $52,000. This was exactly the amount she needed to pay off the balance on her school loans. By taking the time to think about possible solutions, Jill came up with a creative answer to get herself out of debt and relieve herself of stress.

★   Achieving something

When you feel like you brought something to a successful conclusion, made good use of your time, and marked another item off your "to do" list, you boost your self-esteem and self-confidence.

Several members of my family were very good artists, but my sister, Lois, didn't have the same talent. Yet, from the age of four, she told people she was an artist. When she finished high school, she worked as a secretary for many years and in her spare time, she took art classes, attended art shows, and painted pictures. She went back to school at night and studied art, art history, and art education. Eventually, she earned her master's degree in art. At her work, she applied for a transfer to a position as a graphic artist and got the job. She eventually became a very successful artist, designing and painting everything from insignias for NASA to the ceiling of a church in Houston. After her son suffered a severe brain injury from a major motorcycle accident, she took an interest in other children who had been brain-injured. She started a foundation and taught art classes to these children. For the next ten years and until her death, she worked with these children to bring new meaning, self-confidence, and self-respect to their lives. She was passionate about her art and her purpose. Her personal drive and determination drove her to develop her talent. Her creativity, commitment, and caring made a difference in the lives of so many. Teaching these children something she loved and helping them develop self-esteem gave her purpose and made her happy.

★ Serving your community

When you do something you feel improves the lives of your family members, your neighbors, friends or associates, you feel right about it. When we feel right about something, it brings us contentment and joy.

★ Supporting others

When you seize the opportunity to let others know you are there for them, and believe in them as well as their goals and dreams, you are giving them support. When we give support to others, we feel good about ourselves and that makes us happy.

★ Using your talents and abilities

Talents and abilities are our natural endowments. In many cases, we didn't have to work to get them. We were born with them. They are powers and gifts. That's why talented people are often referred to as "gifted." When we use our natural abilities, we are being ourselves; we are being who we were meant to be and not the person someone else thinks we should be. It brings us joy to be ourselves.

I'm happy being me

When I was a child, my mother gave me a small, framed copy of a poem entitled, "I'm Happy Being Me."

Imagine how happy and free I could be

If I took me a little less seriously –

If I'd laugh at my faults every once in a while,

And accept my mistakes with a shrug and a smile,

If I'd take little setbacks and failures in stride,

And remember successes with pleasure and pride –

Imagine how happy and free I could be

If I did all I could to enjoy being me!

The anonymous writer really clarified for me what I needed to do to be happy. From her poem, I learned that even though certain life circumstances may not be good, we can do something about them. We can change our attitudes. We can do something positive. We can choose to be happy and if we do, we'll be free of negative influences and baggage. This little framed, old, tattered poem sits on my desk today and reminds me every day what I need to do to maintain my happiness.

Alfred Lord Tennyson once said, "The happiness of a man in this life does not consist in the absence but in the mastery of his passions."

Find your strengths. Visualize what you want. Pursue it with passion. Listen to your heart. Watch for opportunities. Choose to be happy and tell your face. Get out there and *participate* in life. Believe you can.

Believe You Can Exercise

Make a date with yourself and go somewhere alone. Choose a place that will appeal to your creative side. Stay at least one hour. Do something fun or something brave. Do something you've never done before, or something you have secretly wished you could do. Totally immerse yourself in the expreience.

It might be:

- ✓ Eat lunch in an expensive restaurant
- ✓ Visit a craft store
- ✓ Go to an art gallery
- ✓ Go to the movies
- ✓ Ride the city bus around town
- ✓ Go to the circus
- ✓ Have a picnic in the park
- ✓ Visit a museum
- ✓ Take a helicopter ride over the city

Before you go home, write in your book how you felt while you were doing it. Write about any new experiences or insights you had. Write about any fears and how you felt about yourself when you moved through the fear.

_____

_____

_____

_____

_____

_____

_____

_____

_____

_____

_____

_____

_____

_____

_____

_____

_____

_____

_____

_____

_____

_____

_____

_____

Believe You Can
Affirmation

My passions lead me where I need to be to fulfill my purpose. Every day I gain knowledge and experience. As I live creatively and enthusiastically, I find joy and peace in being me. I am more than enough.

Chapter Seven

Make Life Work for You

The only time to settle for what you have, is when what you have is what you want.

— **NORMAN MONATH**, AUTHOR
KNOW WHAT YOU WANT AND GET IT

Life is what it is and it's up to us to make the best of what we've been given. Even though you may not have the resources or the circumstances you believe you need to improve your life, start with what you have and build the foundation that will allow you to find the resources and change your circumstances. Change doesn't usually happen all at once. It is a process of eliminations and additions until we find the desired direction for our lives.

Give up blame

Blame shifts the responsibility of our lives and our happiness, making it someone else's responsibility. We think, "It's their fault." "They didn't do what they were supposed to do." "They didn't hold up their end of the bargain." "It costs too much." "They talked me into it or out of it." "They prevented me from doing what I wanted to do." The truth is you took the easy way out. You did what you wanted to do at that moment. Maybe you did it because you didn't think about the consequences. Or maybe you chose to buy something you couldn't afford, instead of sticking to your budget. Perhaps you were avoiding an argument or you were scared of the alternative. Whatever the reason, your life is your responsibility.

Stop making excuses

Making excuses is another way we shift responsibility. Instead of blaming people, we blame things or circumstances. "I didn't get it done because the copy machine was broken," or "I couldn't get the repair man out here to look at the machine until next week." Perhaps you could have taken it to a local print shop to have it copied.

My business partner was working on an important project when her copier broke. It was late in the evening and there were no print shops open in the small town where she lived. She called the printer at home and explained her situation to him. He volunteered to come in very early the next morning so she could get her work done in time to meet her deadline. I asked her what she would have done if the printer hadn't agreed to come. She answered, "Then I would have driven 85 miles to the next town where there is a 24-hour copy store near the university and I would have gotten it done there." Where there is a will, there is a way.

Accept responsibility

When we pursue our dreams, often the practical side of us says one thing while the emotional, mental, psychological, or spiritual side says disregard the practical side and go for what you want. We tend to believe we can't follow our hearts or pursue our dreams and still be responsible. That is erroneous thinking.

Nicholas Sparks worked as a pharmaceutical salesman while he wrote his first novel, *The Notebook*. He had a family and responsibilities. He didn't shirk that in order to do his writing. He did both at the same time and he got a $1,000,000 advance for his very first novel.

Learn to live in the present

Instead of being passive, do something about your dream. The present is the only time we have. Think to yourself, "What can I do right now to make my life the best it can be? What one step can I take to advance in a forward direction?"

Start by doing the best you can wherever you are and at whatever you are doing. Years ago, there was a TV commercial that said, "If you had to sign your name to everything you did, would you do it better?" That statement really made an impact on me. Other people observe how you do things. When they see you doing your best, even when you are doing a job you don't like, they'll recognize your commitment to doing a job well and opportunities will start to present themselves. By doing your best at whatever you are doing, you are taking control of the situation.

Allison had a PhD and a powerful job. She thought she deserved to be paid more than she was being paid, so she quit her job. She thought it would be easy to find another job. Months went by and Allison had yet to find a new job. As she had children to feed and other financial obligations, she took a job cleaning other people's houses. Allison is overweight, so hard, physical labor was not easy for her. Regardless, she did it to the best of her ability and was able to pay her bills and meet her obligations while looking for another job that would be more suitable to her skills and education. When one of the people whose home she cleaned commented on the fact that Allison was so happy and pleasant in her work, she laughed and told this woman how she had quit her other job months before and had been unable to find a suitable position at the time. This woman so admired Allison for doing this housekeeping job to the best of her ability and having such a good attitude, even though Allison was extremely overqualified, she recommended Allison to a colleague for a position in the colleague's consulting business. Allison was able to use her knowledge, creative abilities, and expertise in her new job. This led to Allison's successful career as a television personality. When life's circumstances put you in a position where you don't want to be, make the best of it. If you go about your work graciously doing more than is required of you, you will be surprised at the results you will achieve.

If you are unhappy about the situation you are in, know that only you can change it. Do the best you can where you are and take steps to get yourself into a better position as fast as you can. In the meantime, don't complain to others. Complaining will not only make others around you miserable, it will be a constant reminder to you of how miserable you are.

Think of the things you've done today. Did you love what you were doing? Did you do them to the best of your ability? Could you have done anything better? Did you enjoy your day? Did you complain about anything? Did you take any steps to improve your situation?

Become a problem-solver

It is absolutely essential we become problem-solvers. Problem identifiers are a dime a dozen. Anyone can go around pointing out problems. On the other hand, problem-solvers are worth their weight in gold. Far too few people spend their time and use their minds looking for solutions. Problems give us opportunities to be creative. If you can identify a problem, you can certainly use your creative abilities to come up with a possible solution or two.

Don't confuse problem-solving with decision-making. Problem-solving is a brainstorming activity where we look at all the possible options available to us to solve a problem. Decision-making is where we select one of those possibilities. Never make a decision that is not in everyone's best interest. Make your decisions based on what you know is the right thing to do. Be sure what you choose passes the test of your conscience as well as your integrity.

When you see a problem, prepare a careful analysis of that problem and any other problems it may cause. Make sure you are looking at the real problem and not a symptom of a problem. Once you are positive you are addressing the real problem, create a list of possible solutions and recommendations for alternatives. Then evaluate each option to be sure you are doing what is right for all concerned. If you feel in your heart it is the right thing to do, do it!

Remember, if you don't have problems, you aren't growing! Growth is always a creator of problems. These problems are opportunities. A problem just might be the push you need to do something differently.

Make every moment count

Like so many other people, you probably feel your life is moving faster and faster. Today we do everything fast: talk fast, drive fast, even eat fast. Time is at a premium and most of us are afflicted with "hurry sickness." There never seems to be enough time to do the things we have to do, much less those things we'd *like* to do. Many of us don't even have time to think. Something is terribly wrong with this picture. There are probably times when you feel like a spectator watching your own life unfold, instead of being in control. You might even be wondering who you are and what your purpose is!

Time is the most precious and limited resource we have. In spite of our best efforts, time is unyielding. No one can stop it, slow it down, or save it. It is a rare person who has enough time to do all the things she wants to do. If you are like most people, trying to balance a busy professional life and a busy personal life, you know what a challenge it can be to get everything done. Keeping current with what's going on in the world, not to mention technology, your industry, changing expectations at work, and personal obligations, is becoming harder and harder.

For some reason, we keep adding "just one more thing," and forget to eliminate another. The result is an ever-increasing time crunch. Here are some questions for you to consider: "Do I take on too much? Do I have difficulty saying 'No' to extra demands? Do I fail to set priorities? Do I fail to plan?"

Sit back, shut out your other thoughts, and imagine what it would be like to spend your life doing the things which are most important to you. Imagine using your work time on activities that directly relate to achieving your most important goals and to those tasks that must be accomplished and using your personal time to enjoy the things you really want to do. Create a picture in your mind. Envision yourself going through the day doing work that truly makes a difference. It feels good, doesn't it?

Now that you've spent some time exercising your imagination, let's get real. We still have the same amount of time we have always had. The clock still ticks off 24 hours every day. The calendar still has seven days a week, 52 weeks a year. So why do we feel like we are running out of time?

Technology has reshaped the way we work, eat, sleep, play, and live. We are living in an age of instant everything. Information is transmitted at the speed of light and is received instantly. Replies are expected immediately. It seems there is far too much to do and far too little time. You may be asking yourself on a regular basis, "How can I get all this done in the time I have?" or, "Is this all there is to life?" It's possible you are feeling less and less satisfaction, as well as more and more stress. People in this predicament often say, "I need to manage my time more effectively." or "I need to get control of my time." Realize this! You can't manage or control time. No one can. *You can only manage yourself and your activities* within the time you have.

Women who are in positions of power are usually excellent self-managers. They have learned to set priorities, delegate effectively, and make decisions quickly, all of which are parts of managing themselves. If you want to dramatically improve the overall quality of your life, you must learn to manage yourself.

Joan Baez once said, "You don't get to choose how you are going to die or when. You can only decide how you're going to live."

Decide right now that you are going to start making every moment of your life count. To my knowledge, this is the only life you are going to get, so make it enjoyable, satisfying, and rewarding. There are three primary aspects to doing this: take control, work smarter, and take action.

Step #1 Take control

Taking control begins with analyzing what really happens to your time. Keep a time log for a period of two weeks in order to see exactly what you do with your time. Make a thorough analysis. When you do this, it will identify time-wasters and all activities that are not necessary, as well as where you are spending time that doesn't contribute to your goals. You will, of course, also identify time spent on areas that are getting the best results. You are probably thinking, "I don't have time to keep a time log. That's just one more thing that will add stress to my life." Stop it. That is negative. Just do it! In two weeks, you'll be glad you did, as you will no doubt be amazed at what you discover!

A highly successful director in the hospitality industry was at a point of burnout when she attended one of our seminars. She was working six or seven days every week, 12 to 14 hours per day and had not taken a break or vacation for six years. She was earning a lot of money, but was extremely unfit and overweight. The continuous hard work over the years was taking its toll on her, both physically and mentally. She most certainly wasn't enjoying life and had very little fulfillment.

After attending our program, she began to analyze her time and she realized how much of what she was doing was not contributing to what she had originally set out to accomplish. She immediately began to set new goals in her life so she could utilize her time with activities that would help her accomplish those goals. Within six months, she had literally turned her life around. When she began refocusing her energies on what worked and simplifying her activities, she was able to spend more time with her family and do the things that were most important to her. She began to exercise regularly and lose weight, which gave her more energy. With her increased focus on what was really important, she was able to improve business results with very little effort **and** take more time off. She learned the difference between working harder and working smarter.

It really does pay to analyze what you do with your time!

Step #2 Work smarter

Make a time log with six columns. Title these six columns: *Time, Activity, Value, Urgent, Scheduled,* and *Interruption.* Every half hour, write in the time and then enter what you have just done in the Activity column. In the Value column, which determines whether or not a particular activity contributes to your established goals, indicate the value by entering a plus sign which means yes, it is of value, or a minus sign which means no, it's not. Then place a check mark in the Urgent column if there is any follow-up activity that has an upcoming deadline. Make a check mark in the Scheduled column if the activity was pre-planned. Place a check mark in the Interruption column if this activity was an unexpected interruption.

Time	Activity	Value	Urgent	Scheduled	Interruption

You will realize from keeping this time log that there is an enormous number of activities, which are not contributing to the achievement of your goals. By the time you have made a thorough analysis of everything you do, you will decide to do more of some activities and less of others. You will probably even *stop* doing certain activities entirely and *start* doing others.

After two weeks, make an in-depth analysis of your time log. This involves looking at each column and asking yourself various questions:

1. ***Activity column*** Which activities can be simplified? Which ones can be delegated or even eliminated? Which ones need more attention? Which ones did you enjoy doing?

2. ***Value column*** What percentage of your activities were of value?

3. ***Urgent column*** What percentage were really urgent? Were they also important? What percentage could have been taken care of sooner so they could have avoided becoming urgent?

4. ***Scheduled column*** What percentage were planned or expected?

5. ***Interruption column*** What percentage were interruptions? Who or what was your most frequent interrupter? How were you interrupted most often — phone, email, or in person? Were they necessary interruptions? Were you comfortable with how you handled them?

Are there major differences between what you hoped to accomplish and what you actually did achieve? Are you spending your time pursuing those things that have high value to you? If not, why not?

Set your priorities

Plan yearly, quarterly, monthly, weekly, and daily. The secret to successful planning is to allow extra time for unexpected situations and not over-commit or over-book yourself. Establish priorities for your activities so that at the end of the day, you will have completed the most important things. Planning long projects and breaking them down into smaller projects and timetables will help you dedicate a few minutes each day to important high-value activities that carry future due dates. By getting ahead on projects, you are less likely to have last minute crises and time crunches.

The following five questions will help improve your time utilization:

1. Did my activity relate directly to one or more of my goals or objectives?

2. How can my activities be better handled in the future?

3. What activities can I delegate in the future and to whom?

4. What activities will I eliminate because they are useless?

5. Which activities can I minimize or control the time involvement?

Beware of bad habits that can sabotage your best efforts. Subconscious patterns can make you your own worst enemy. Whether it is trying to remember everything instead of making lists, being consistently late because you wanted to do just one more thing before leaving the office, or being easily distracted, you can change your habits.

A lot of people believe they can multi-task. Actually, what people are doing is interrupting one task with another. It is nearly impossible to do things well when you are trying to do many things at the same time.

Make decisions quickly

Once you have all of the available facts, make a decision. Rarely does delay improve the quality of choice. Over-analysis can be seductive and stress-producing. Keep in mind that nearly all decisions must be made with imperfect information. That's why it is called a "decision." If you make a decision and you don't get the outcome you want, don't beat yourself up. Realize that you have found one more way that doesn't work and make another decision. Just keep adjusting until you do get the outcome you want.

In his book, *Think and Grow Rich*, Napoleon Hill wrote "Analysis of over 25,000 men and women who had experienced failure disclosed the fact that lack of decision-making was near the head of the list of the thirty-one major causes of failure. Procrastination, the opposite of decision, is a common enemy which practically everyone must conquer."

Delegate regularly

If you have a staff or employees, delegate to them. If done right, delegation is a learning experience and a motivator. Actively look for things your staff does well and let them do it. Employees are more often limited by our abilities than theirs. A manager or supervisor is supposed to spend only 20 percent of her time actually performing tasks herself and the other 80 percent of the time managing and supervising. Most of the executives we've counseled were doing just the opposite. I can't count the number of times managers have said to me, "Well, by the time I explained it to them, I could have done it myself." You might feel that way, too, but as long as you keep doing the work yourself, no one else gets trained and you will have to keep on doing it. When you are in a management or supervisory position, it is your job to get work done through other people. They don't need to do the job exactly like you would, and the odds are they won't. Explain to them the result or outcome you want and let them do their jobs. Ask them to make a plan and go over it with you before they begin. If their plan is workable, let them do the job their way.

Recently, our office copy machine broke down and when the repairman came to look at it, he said, "It's finished." In the old days, I would have gone out and researched state-of-the-art copy machines and eventually bought the best model that the salesman demonstrated to me. This is very time-consuming. Besides, I'm not the one who uses the copy machine the most. This time I decided to let the person who uses the machine select and order it. It empowered her and it saved me a great deal of time and money. She was much more cost-conscious than I would have been. In addition, she received the training on the machine and knows how to use it, which means I am not going to be the one getting interrupted to answer questions about it. The biggest and best advantage is that since she has been trained on this new machine, she has taken over all of the copying. This is saving me even more time!

Learn to delegate at home, too

Your husband or partner and children are good candidates for your delegation skills. Empower them to make some decisions, give them the responsibility of keeping particular rooms clean or doing certain tasks.

Don't do it for them. Remember, if you make yourself a doormat to the world, you can't blame everyone for wiping their feet on you. When the job is completed, reward them for a job well done, just the same as you would your employees.

Effective self-management offers many rewards in your business and personal life. When you accomplish your goals and priorities, you are awarded greater freedom. It becomes easier to relax, because there is no guilt about what might be left undone. Effective self-management may result in a lightened workload, career advancement, and an increase in efficiency, effectiveness, and productivity. It will even improve your relationships!

Step #3 Take action

Oliver Wendell Holmes said, "I find the great thing in this world is not so much where we stand as in what direction we are moving. To reach the port of Heaven, we must sail sometimes with the wind and sometimes against it, but we must sail and not drift nor lie at anchor." Action is our only choice. Without it, we become stagnant and like a ship at anchor, we'll go nowhere. We must take specific, directed action to reach our destination.

Control interruptions, time-wasters, and distractions

Whether you are at work, at home, or in a home-based business, interruptions and distractions can be treacherous. Look for patterns in interruptions. Often, they are caused by ineffective systems or a breakdown in the system, process, or function. Low-priority items often masquerade as important things because they require your immediate attention. However, they will often take care of themselves without your intervention. Consider this example: When you are on vacation, you aren't there to handle all the things that need to be handled. Somehow everything manages to get taken care of. But of course, even on vacation, emergencies and urgent matters do come up that need your immediate attention. Treat your day-to-day work activities the same way — deal only with the most important and urgent matters and leave the mundane for another time, if at all.

Discipline your daily habits

No matter what you do, discipline is the key to success. If you want to finish school, lose weight, write a book, become a singer, save money, be organized or be productive, you must have good daily habits. Success is a result of diligent and deliberate discipline every day.

Sure, I understand there are many things you have to do that take up your time. Your bed still needs to be made, dinner still needs to be cooked for the family, your husband still needs to hear you love him, especially when you are showing signs of growth and change, but you must stay focused and set aside time to do something toward your goals every day. Every step, no matter how big or small, is one step closer to the life you desire.

Develop your skills

Learn as much as you can about whatever it is you decide to do. Educate yourself. If you can't afford a formal education, read books. Libraries are full of them and it doesn't cost you anything to go there and read or to check them out and take them home. The Internet is a very useful tool. Nearly everything you could possibly want to know can be found on the Internet. If you don't know how, immediately learn to use it.

Continue gathering knowledge and information throughout your life. Every day you are either getting better or you are getting worse. Nothing stays the same. The world is constantly evolving. You must do the same.

Continue to grow

There is no reason why you should ever stop growing. We should do something every day to expand our minds. Many of us stop learning because we let our imaginations lie dormant. We don't use them. Also, we let negativity creep in. Often people say, "I'm too old," or "The competition is too great." If you think you are too old, you should meet my friend, Dominic's, mother. She is 92, healthy, happy, and still works as a legal secretary. She has been in this position with this firm for more than 50 years. She stays vital, vibrant, and alive because she has purpose and passion for what she does. She continues to enjoy her quality of life long after many have given up.

Practice life-long learning

Just because you have gotten this far doesn't mean you have all the knowledge, skills, and ability you need to survive and thrive in the world. People want to know what you have done lately. You are never as far as you can go. There is no finish line! Use your imagination. No matter what circumstances we are in or what age we are, we can keep creating better conditions. Even if it's just one percent better than yesterday, it's a step forward. If you keep this in mind and practice this approach, you will find that every day, every month and every year you will be advancing. Set your sights on the greatest goal you can think of and hold it in your mind. Whether it is experience, an advance degree, a certification, or winning a trophy, keep going. Keep learning. Become the best you can be at whatever you are doing, whether it's being a parent, working at a trade or in a service position, or conditioning your body. Do it to the best of your ability.

Pace yourself

Have you ever watched a mountain goat climb a mountain? At one time, I lived in the mountains and it was a wonderful experience to watch one of our bighorn sheep as it climbed up a mountain. He would climb for a while and when he reached a ledge, he rested. He'd look around, walk around the mountain at the same level for a while and then start to climb again, but not straight up. He went at an angle, working his way around the rocks and the brush. Sometimes, he came back down a bit, went across and started up again, stopping along the way to graze or rest.

We can learn a lot from the bighorn. If we want to reach our goal, we need to stop every now and then to look around, check out where we are, where the path is taking us, and see if there are any obstacles we are going to need to go around. It may be longer to go around, but perhaps the benefits of that path are better. Sometimes we may have to go back down a bit in order to take a different path which will take us closer to our goal. Most of us don't like to backtrack, but it can be a necessary step in accomplishing our goals. We need to nurture ourselves, rest when we are tired, and pace ourselves. Otherwise, we may burn out along the way.

Eliminate unnecessary and inappropriate activities

Don't attempt to jam more and more activities into your already over-crowded schedule. Learn to say no to things that don't fit in with your goals. If you say "Yes" to everything, then "Yes" doesn't mean much when it's said. Saying "No" more often allows you to say "Yes" to your priorities and to really important things. It will allow you to participate fully when you do say "Yes."

Identify those areas of greatest stress and begin to make changes. A continual high stress, high-rush style can cause health problems, not to mention sleep and interpersonal difficulties.

Take care of your body

You must pace yourself in order to maintain your health. A person in great health emits attractiveness, energy, and effervescence. That's because her body is full of strength, energy, and well-being. Good health adds strength and vitality to your personality. You feel better able to deal with situations and people when your health is good.

If you don't feel well, you certainly won't feel like dealing with difficult situations or difficult people. It is hard to be pleasant, charming, and exciting when you are sick. It is difficult to think, much less make decisions, when you aren't feeling well.

Start now to create the kind of health that puts color in your skin, a sparkle in your eyes, and a skip in your walk. These are the characteristics of a charismatic personality.

I'm sure you've been at a meeting that was just dragging along when some dynamic person entered and the meeting took on a new life. Or perhaps you were feeling rather bored and unexcited about your life when you heard a speaker deliver a dynamic presentation. You felt as though he or she was speaking directly to you and you came away inspired and full of new energy. Maybe a person across the room caught your interest even before you had the opportunity to shake hands. Much of that attraction is physical. Having great health adds vitality to your personality and will attract people to you.

Recharge your battery

What happens when you feel like your battery is dead and you just can't go on? Do you give up and say, "Oh well, I didn't want to go to that destination anyway?" or, "That's just my luck. I've never been able to reach my goals?"

At one time or another, most of us seem to run low on energy. This happens when things aren't going the way we expected or we have worked too long and too hard without achieving our desired results. This is a critical time. This is not the time to give up. It is the time to take a break, go to the spa, go home and not answer the telephone or the door, go on a drive in the country, walk in the grass barefooted, have a picnic with someone really special, or go on vacation. Whatever you do, make sure it is something you enjoy. Your brain needs time to process everything that is currently going on without any additional input.

Commitment

Your goals have more chance of becoming a reality when you are committed to them. Many people talk about how committed they are, but when push comes to shove, they quit. Real commitment means you don't give up until you achieve the desired result.

Even when an obstacle gets in your way or you have a setback, you never give up. Committed people understand there is a price to pay to achieve anything worthwhile. Find out the risks and rewards before you decide to follow a path. It will be easier to keep your commitments when you know what to expect before you make the agreement.

Many of us are very good at keeping commitments to other people. We raise our children, make dinner, attend functions, organize the car pool, clean the house, do the laundry, do community volunteer work, and in addition, pursue our careers. We put everyone else's priorities ahead of our own. We make promises to ourselves that we don't keep. We provide excuses such as I was too busy, my boss needed me, I had to go to the children's school function, my husband needed it done for him, and all the while that little voice inside of us says, "What about me? Don't I deserve some attention as well?" When we don't keep the commitments we make to ourselves, we feel hurt, frustrated, resentful, and unworthy.

Part of the reason we don't keep our commitments to ourselves is that we have been conditioned to look after others first. We can't indefinitely continue to place commitments to others ahead of our own without damaging our self-esteem and ultimately our relationships. It is not selfish, self-centered, or egotistical to keep our commitments to ourselves. When we feel a sense of accomplishment, we will have more energy and be more willing to give to others.

Give to someone else

We are living in the "me" generation. I'll help you if I get something out of it. "You scratch my back and then I'll scratch yours." Many people today are living for themselves. They don't want to help other people. They focus on their own wants, needs, and expectations. When they are in trouble or they need assistance, they wonder why they can't find anyone to help.

If you truly want to be happy and fulfilled, learn to give as well as take. When you find yourself getting discouraged or depressed, it's usually when you are all caught up in yourself. When you go out and help someone else, you'll get your mind off your own problems. When you make a difference in someone else's life, it will make a difference in yours.

When I hear people say how lonely they are, I want to shake them and say, "There are a lot of people out there who could use your company. Quit feeling sorry for yourself. Get off your rear and go see if you can cheer them up." There are hundreds of people in retirement centers, convalescent homes, hospitals, and orphanages who would like a visitor. You probably have a friend or know someone somewhere who has a need for someone to listen to her right now. There are neighbors who need their lawns mowed or shut-ins who could use some food. There are people who have lost loved ones and would appreciate someone holding their hands. If the only thing you have to give is a smile, give that to someone. There are so many people out there who could use a smile, a hug, or even a kind word. Jesus said, "If you even give so much as a cup of water to someone in need, I see it and I'm going to reward you."

Give without expecting to receive a reward. Give from your heart and what you receive will be satisfaction and peace of mind. If you have not seen the movie, *Pay It Forward*, rent it and watch it. The message of doing for another who then will do for someone else, is powerful.

Make your life make a difference. Dr. Martin Luther King said, "Greatness is determined by service." We all have greatness within us.

Make Your Life Work Exercise

Schedule an hour with yourself. Put it on your appointment calendar. Go someplace where you will not be interrupted. Turn off your cell phone and use the time to make a contract with yourself.

Write what you agree to do to achieve your dreams. This is an agreement with yourself only. It is a formal contract, not a list of wishes and hopes. Your level of achievement will be determined by your level of commitment. State it, sign it, and date it.

Commitment to Myself

I, _____, do hereby declare and affirm that I am committed to my success. Now, therefore, I pledge to do the following:

_____

_____

_____

Signature_____ Date_____

My Life Works Affirmation

My life works. I am committed to my success. I dedicate my energy, my knowledge, and my skills to myself and my goals. I use what I have and do what I need to do to move forward. I take charge, take action, and take responsibility for my life. I am more than enough.

Chapter Eight

Say What You Mean and Sound Like You Mean It

... in the end, the communicator will be confronted with the old problem of what to say and how to say it.

— **EDWARD R. MURROW**
AMERICAN BROADCAST JOURNALIST

Working with women throughout the world has shown me that no matter how successful women are becoming, many of us still find ourselves feeling powerless and frustrated in our interactions with others.

In recent years, we have heard much about the differences in how women and men communicate and we have been encouraged to communicate more like men. As a woman who has been in senior management in one of the world's largest media groups, as well as an entrepreneur, I have learned it is not always necessary to communicate using the words and styles of our male counterparts. We simply need to use a direct form of communication and be very clear about what we are saying. We must stand up for our beliefs and speak out, instead of holding things inside. As young girls, many of us were conditioned to be docile, submissive, and dependent, while our brothers were expected to be adventurous, daring, strong, and independent. That is not the style we need today.

Self-acceptance

The very first thing we need to do to become persuasive communicators is to learn to communicate with ourselves in a positive manner. We need to learn to use kind words with ourselves. You wouldn't tell your best friends they are stupid, ugly, dumb, or you wish the floor would swallow them up. So why do we talk to ourselves in that manner? It is our responsibility to create a place for ourselves to feel self-acceptance. It is **not** okay to talk negatively to ourselves. Don't demand perfection of yourself. Be honest with yourself about your feelings. Feelings of inadequacy are usually triggered by something, someone, or some situation from the past. You are not dealing with the past now. Remain in the moment. You are only dealing with the situation you are in at this time. It is important to learn to cope with situations, rather than feeling like you have to defend yourself or your position. Cool heads prevail. Your responsibility is to act in a way that makes you feel better, not worse.

When we feel good about ourselves, it becomes easier to show respect for other people. In demonstrating this respect for them, we show them we value them.

Relationships, responsibilities, and roles

Remember to consider the relationship, your responsibility to the relationship, and the role you play within it. Every interaction with another person is a relationship, whether it is with family members, co-workers, subordinates, bosses, friends, or associates. How much does this relationship mean to you? How much could it mean? It is important for all parties involved in any relationship to feel like it is a win-win. It is important for everyone to keep their self-esteem intact. What is more important . . . the relationship, or being right about a particular point? You need to be clear about your objectives and your desired outcomes before you enter into any discussion or interaction.

What is your responsibility? My mother would sometimes say, "You are bigger than the way you are acting." And I would think, "Well, I don't want to be bigger. I want to win." What I had to learn was "behaving bigger" meant behaving in a way that showed respect to the other people in the relationship or situation - and myself as well. If I made the choice to give respect, I would fulfill my responsibility and come out a winner.

To show respect, I had to learn to take 100 percent responsibility for the communication process.

When we are speaking, we need to make sure that we are clear and concise. When we are listening, we must be sure we hear what is said and what is meant. If we don't understand something, we should ask the speaker to clarify the meaning for us. Stick with the process and continue to question until you understand each other.

What is your role? Make the choice to be the one to take the first step toward satisfactory communication and create a more cohesive relationship or environment. After all, what is your objective? It is to communicate effectively.

Powerful communication

Your communication style is simply a series of behaviors. You have the power to choose words and behaviors to communicate the message you want to send. Ask yourself, "Is the way I am communicating now aiding or hindering my relationships? Is my behavior aiding or hindering whether or not I am trusted or respected? Am I showing them respect? Am I showing that I value them? Am I getting the results I want in my life? If I'm not, why not? Which of my behaviors do I need to change?"

Miscommunication is the number one problem in most organizations today. It is also the number one problem in most homes and most relationships. "Why is it so difficult?" Consider this; there are eight realities about our communication that exists at any one time.

★ What I mean to say

★ What I actually do say

★ What you heard me say

★ What you thought you heard me say

★ What you mean to say

★ What you actually do say

★ What I heard you say

★ What I thought I heard you say

No wonder we misunderstand each other! Quality communication only happens when the intent of the message is understood.

Communicate for understanding

Stephen Covey states in his book, *The 7 Habits of Highly Effective People*, Habit #5, "Seek first to understand and then to be understood." Two ways in which we can seek to understand are by *asking* questions and *listening* to what is being said.

When attempting to communicate with another person, don't just assume you understood. Clarify instead. Ask questions until you know what you heard and understood was indeed what the other person meant.

We never know what other people are thinking or feeling. Even if they tell us, we can't fully experience their feeling, because it isn't happening to us. We don't have the same background, experiences, upbringing, or memories they have. Even if we are experiencing the same thing now, our perception of it is probably totally different.

By assuming we understand, we might actually cause other people to be defensive. Don't say things like, "I know exactly how you feel." You don't know how they feel. You aren't them. Their feelings are different than yours. You will never fully understand how they feel.

Don't jump in and start telling the other person about a similar thing that happened to you. First, show some compassion.

Ask open-ended questions

Open-ended questions start with the words, "Who, what, when, where, which, how, and why." Be careful with your use of "Why." It could sound like you are placing blame. "Why did you do it that way?" or "Why did you make that choice?" said with the wrong tone of voice can be asking for a fight. Instead, ask who will be affected by their decisions, what they would like to see done differently, when is their deadline, where they can get the resources they might need and how you can support them. Then listen to their answers.

Then, and only then, if your story applies to the situation, ask if they'd like to hear about a time when you were in a similar situation and what you did about it. If they say, "Yes," then they are really interested in what you have to say. Too many times we start solving the other person's problem or telling them how they should handle it, could handle it, or how we would have handled it when all they wanted us to do was listen. Listening and then asking questions shows we care and we value the other person and her thoughts, ideas, and opinions.

One evening in South Africa, Vimmi, took me to dinner with a group of his friends. The lady sitting to my right was Afrikaans and spoke with a heavy accent. At one point, she leaned over to me and almost whispered, "I'm a kangaroo." Not ever having had dinner with a kangaroo before, I didn't know what to say, so I said, "That's nice." A little while later, she said it again. My mind was going crazy. I wanted to ask, "How did you get to Africa?" "Why did you leave Australia?" "What do you have in your pouch?" or "How far can you hop?" But all I said was, "That's nice." She continued to make the statement that she was a kangaroo throughout the evening and I became more and more uncomfortable.

Later when we were walking to the car, Vimmi asked me what was wrong with me that all I said all evening was, "That's nice." I told him I had never before been around anyone who thought she was a kangaroo, and I didn't quite know how to deal with the situation. He started to laugh and said, "She didn't say she was a kangaroo. She said she came from the Karoo. The Karoo is our desert and you came from the desert in America. She was attempting to start a conversation with something you have in common."

If I had just asked what I was thinking, it would have clarified the situation right then and there. I'm sure we both would have had a good laugh and a more comfortable and pleasant evening.

Listen aggressively

People have a desire and a need to be listened to and be heard. It is important to ask questions and comment on what they have said. When we jump in and start telling our story without showing interest in them, it doesn't say, "I listened." It sounds more like "I can top that."

Listen without interrupting. Listen without making judgments. Listen to be sure you understand what they are saying and what they are feeling. You aren't listening when you're thinking of what you're going to say next, formulating a clever retort, making judgments, keeping score, or arguing in your mind. Listening is a three-step process:

Step #1 Attending

This means to be attentive. Stop what you're doing, look at the other person, and give him or her your undivided attention.

Step #2 Following

Follow along with what is being said by making one or two-word comments from time-to-time. At the very least, nod your head. Affirm you are listening by saying, "Really?" "Is that so?" or "I understand." This will convey that you are actively listening to what the other person is saying.

Step #3 Paraphrasing

Paraphrase or repeat back what you understood the other person to say. Be sure to repeat back both the words you heard the person say and the feelings you understood the person to have. Don't repeat the exact words in parrot fashion. Instead start with something like, "It sounds to me like you are saying you're angry because . . . ," "What I'm understanding you to say is that you are frustrated with . . . ," or "Let me make sure I'm understanding the situation. What I understood you are concerned with is . . ." Then finish the sentence by paraphrasing or summarizing your understanding of what was said and felt. Don't add the word *but* here. "What I understood you to say was . . . but in my opinion . . ." When you say *but*, it takes away the value of your expression of understanding. It can even sound as though you are correcting the other person. A woman attending one of my seminars spoke up and said proudly, "I don't use *but*; I use *however.*" Understand this. The word *however* is simply a dressed-up *but*. It means the same thing as *but* and so do *nevertheless*, *yet*, and *although*. Negative words have no benefit. Lose them. They discount whatever you have said before. "You are a wonderful person, *but* . . . ," "I value what you did, *however . . . ,*" "You handled that well, *yet. . . .*" As you can see, you don't even have to finish those sentences! Those words take away any positive meaning from your statement.

Use *and* instead of *but.* It does two things. First, it maintains, instead of negating, the other person's value, action, or idea. Second, it gives you a chance to steer or correct the other person while being supportive. *But* makes the listener think, "Uh-oh, what's coming next?" We show others we care by the words we use. Focus on the positive. Replace the words, *have to* with *could,* replace *always* with *often,* replace *I can't* with *Let me see what I **can** do.*

Even in disagreement, we can show people we value them. Instead of starting sentences with the word, *you,* start your sentences with *I.* "*I am understanding you to say . . .* " Instead of using words like *angry, mad* or *frustrated,* use the words *concerned* or *surprised.* Instead of "*You make me so angry,*" say "*I am concerned that . . . ,*" or "*I was surprised when you . . .*" The use of more positive words in your vocabulary will show the other person you care and give that person a feeling of trust when communicating with you. Plus, owning your feelings doesn't put other people on the defensive for their actions. You are simply sharing how you feel about something.

You can never build relationships by using words that annihilate, devastate, or annoy another person. Anthony Robbins, the author of *Unlimited Power,* says, "The quality of your communication determines the quality of your life."

Attitude adjustments needed

In a recent seminar, a young lady raised her hand and said, "People around here think I have a bad attitude. I don't have a bad attitude. I'm just not a morning person." Have you noticed that people who are not morning people usually aren't afternoon people either? They have just developed a bad habit. I suggested she get up a few hours earlier so she could have her afternoons while the others in her office are having their mornings. In that way, she could change their perception of her. Just because you aren't at your peak performance in the morning doesn't mean you have the right to act miserably and be rude to people around you.

What is attitude?

Attitude is an outward expression of an inner feeling. You communicate your attitude by the behaviors you demonstrate to others. The demonstration of your attitude is a choice. We either choose to act in a manner others perceive as positive or in a manner others perceive as negative. Attitudes come from how we communicate with ourselves. If we say to ourselves that we are "not a morning person," then we have conditioned our minds to believe exactly that. If, on the other hand, we say, "I wake up alert and excited every morning," then we condition our minds to perceive our situation in a positive manner. What we think about is what we bring about.

When you think of yourself as a valuable asset to the world, you will be. Your communication with others is based on your perception of yourself. How you see yourself is how you relate and project. Your image of yourself shapes your behavior, thus shaping your communication with others.

How you put your information across, no matter what time of day it is, will determine your outcomes. Communication is directly related to perceptions. Think in terms of who you are communicating with, what perception you want them to have of you, what image you are creating in their minds, and how they perceive your present attitude.

Positioning information

There are two ways you become strong, powerful, respected, impressive, and successful. First, position your information. Communication is most effective when it is purposefully positioned. When you say the right thing at the right time using the right tone of voice, the right facial expressions, and the right body language, you will get the right response. Be consciously aware of how you sound, what you say, and how you look when you say it.

Second, perception is the other person's reality. If you want to be perceived as powerful, get rid of the intensive adverbs in your communication style. These include such modifiers as *just, terribly, such, awfully, quite, probably,* and *kind of.* These are known as hedgers or softeners. *That was quite interesting.* Was it interesting or not? *He was probably wrong.* Why would you say someone was wrong unless you knew for sure he was wrong? Eliminate words from your vocabulary that have no apparent semantic intent; for example, *well, you know, like, if you know what I mean,* and *okey-dokey.*

Don't drop letters

Many of us have fallen into the sloppy habit of dropping the last letters from words in our speech. We say *somethin'* instead of something; *d'ya* instead of do you; *d'ju* instead of Did you; *didn chew* instead of didn't you; *wanna* instead of want to, *ax* instead of ask, *fatha* instead of father; *ridin* instead of riding; and *slep* instead of slept.

Listen to yourself. Listen to other people. Do you sound educated? It's important to pronounce words, including the last letters, clearly and distinctly. Practice finishing one word before you start to speak the next one.

Sometimes we also mispronounce the middle portion of words such as: *lekcher* instead of lecture, *edjacation* instead of education, *chocklit* instead of chocolate, and *pitcher* instead of picture. Losing middle syllables can sound just as bad as losing the last letter.

Certain misuses of words give away your cultural background and education, or lack of one. Be careful not to say, *dees* instead of these," "*doze* instead of those, *liddle* instead of little, *budder* instead of butter, *you guys* instead of you, *learned* when you mean taught. I remember hearing it said that when a man refers to *the wife,* instead of "my wife," it is an indication of a poor cultural background.

When I was traveling in China, our interpreter asked me what the American word *jeat* meant. As I had never heard it before, I asked him to spell it. He said that he didn't spell very well in English, but thought it was "G-E-E-T." I told him I didn't believe I had ever heard it, and asked him to tell me how the tourists used it. He said it was predominantly people from Texas who used it, and they said the word by itself. When I returned home from China, I told my sister about it and she started smiling. Then she said, "*Jeat yet?*" I still didn't get it. Then she repeated slowly, "*Did you eat yet?*" Of course! When said very fast to a person who doesn't speak English as a first language, it probably sounds like *Geet* or *Jeat.* When you don't speak proper English, it becomes harder for people, no matter what their culture, to understand what you are trying to say.

Slang, vulgarities, and curse words

In today's conversation, slang, vulgarities, and curse words seem to sneak unnoticed into many people's vocabularies. That is, unnoticed by the person speaking, not the person listening. Listeners definitely notice. If you habitually use these words, one of them will pop out of your mouth at the wrong time one day . . . probably at the very moment you are trying to impress someone. It'll certainly make an impression, but not the kind you want.

Become aware of words and phrases you use on a daily basis. Phrases such as, *it's my guess that, by the way, in the interim,* and *perhaps so* make you seem unsure of what you are saying. At the same time, there are phrases that have been so poorly used in general that now their use will identify you as a lesser-educated person. Examples of these are: *you know, if you know what I mean, you said it, you betcha, no worries, no sweat, duh,* and *that sort of stuff.*

When used as an idiom, slang is well-accepted and does have a purpose in our communication, but too much slang can be annoying and distracting from the conversation. Eliminate words and phrases from your vocabulary such as *cool, awesome, sweet, hot, bad, baloney, shoot the breeze, blow your top, flip your lid,* and *knocked me for a loop.*

Some women use curse words to make themselves seem stronger to others or to indicate they mean business. You can be very powerful without ever using vulgarities. In fact, I have never heard a curse word from one of the most powerful women I know. She is the chairman of the board of a group of companies listed on the stock exchange and is always able to make herself fully understood without using words that are likely to be offensive. People know what kind of power she has.

Never talk on a subject or say words that offend those who hear you, whether you are talking directly to them or they happen to be within hearing distance. When my assistant was in the bookstore recently, she reached across a table to pick up a book at the same time another woman reached for it. The woman said, "You are a real b . . ." My assistant was so surprised, she jumped backwards and released her hold on the book. As it turned out, the woman was talking to someone on her telephone, but from where my assistant was standing she couldn't see the headset.

In traveling with other professionals, I have been surprised at the number of times I have heard the intimate details of their sexual experiences. Whether you are married or not, sex is a personal and private relationship between you and your partner and should not be shared with the world at large.

Shunt remarks

People often use statements like, *I heard that* ... , *Everyone knows* ..., *They say* ... *They tell me* ... , or, *It's reported that* ... It's possible you even use some of them. The use of these phrases indicates you are unspecific, haven't done your homework, and are the kind of person who starts rumors.

You always want to sound educated, knowledgeable, and prepared — especially in business. It gives you credibility.

Giggling

Don't fill silence or try to cover up embarrassing moments with giggling. It says you are immature and unprofessional. If something is truly funny and it is appropriate to laugh, then laugh. If it is embarrassing, either apologize or don't say anything.

Tag lines

A statement relays knowledge. When it is followed by a tagline, it implies lack of confidence in yourself, doubt in your information, or suggests you are not certain of what you should be doing. It is as though we are asking for confirmation rather than making a firm declaration. "We should really get those contracts signed today, *shouldn't we?*" or "That's the right amount, *isn't it?*" This language can give others the impression we are indecisive. It might seem as though you could be persuaded to give in to the opinions of others, or you are leaving yourself a way to get out of the situation if no one else agrees with you. "We've been debating this issue long enough, *haven't we?*" How much confidence do you have in a person who sounds uncertain or without conviction?

Disqualifiers

When you make a statement or express your opinion, don't disqualify what you say by putting a tag line on the front of the sentence.

Maybe I shouldn't mention this, but . . .
I'm sorry, but . . .
This could be a bit premature, but . . .
I probably shouldn't say this, but . . .
This may not be a good idea, but . . .

Don't preface statements of fact with *I think, I feel,* or *I believe,* when it is the truth about the situation. We sometimes tend to do this when we don't want to sound too aggressive. Don't weaken your position by using these tag lines. When I was in senior management in a large organization, I said to the CEO, "I feel we should . . ." and before I got any further, he said, "Ms. Moreo, at this level we don't pay you to feel, we pay you to know. Do you know or don't you?" I don't have to tell you how I felt about his statement. After that, whenever I had a statement of fact to make, I just made it. State your opinions and make your suggestions directly.

Say, *Let's get with the car dealership and do a car give-away,* rather than *Well, I think maybe we could contact the car dealership that might be persuaded to participate in a promotion where we might be able to hold a raffle and possibly give away a car. I feel the dealership might do it.* This type of talk is known as "spilling," and it goes on so long other people quit listening.

Stay away from lightweight descriptions also known as faint, withering praise, such as, "That was rather good," or "That was a fairly accurate report." What does *rather good* mean? Is it good or isn't it? What is fairly accurate? Is it accurate or not? If the other person says she didn't like it or it wasn't accurate, are you then going to turn around and say, "That's what I meant?"

When you want someone to do something, don't phrase it as a request, unless you are prepared to hear "No." It minimizes your position when you soften instructions this way. *I was wondering if you would . . . ?* or *If you're not too busy, could you . . .? Do you think you might be able to . . . ?* or *Could you possibly . . . ?* If you are asking a subordinate to take action, this is a dangerous tactic. Usually, it won't get done and if it does, she believes you owe her a favor in return.

Asking for approval when you don't really need it also weakens your credibility and your authority. *If it's okay with you I am going to . . .* What if it's not okay with her? Are you then *not* going to do whatever it was you were going to do? *May I interrupt you for a minute?* You already interrupted when you asked that question. Just say, "Excuse me."

Interruptions

When interrupted, speak up. Don't just sit there and pout. Actually say, *Please let me finish*, or, *Excuse me; I wasn't finished*. If the other person is very aggressive, you may want to put your hand out to indicate *Stop*, and then say, *I'd like to hear your opinion when I am finished making my point.* Don't smile when you do this. I am a big supporter of smiles, but not during any kind of conflict. Smiles must be appropriate to the situation.

Build your personality

Personality is a very difficult word to define. It is your individuality. It is what makes you unique. If you have a pleasant personality, people will be attracted to you. If you have a difficult personality and are constantly interrupting others, contradicting them, and trying to show them how wrong they are, you certainly won't make people like or respect you.

I have heard it said we don't have to like the people with whom we work; we just have to show them respect. I agree with that. I also know that work is a lot easier and a lot more fun when we can do it with people we like. As you know only too well, life is not always the way we would prefer it to be. Basically, we all have a deep-seated need to be liked, to have approval, and to belong. It's natural. Don't try to cover it up and say, "I don't care if anyone likes me or not," because you do care.

Aspects of personality

Your personality has three aspects: *physical, mental,* and *spiritual*. Each one of these expands with new experiences, new interests, and new contacts. Each of these three aspects will change many times in your life. You are not the same person now that you were a few years ago and you won't remain as you are now.

Don't say, *People just don't like me and there's nothing I can do about it*, or *I'm not attractive and that's all there is to it*. You are in control of any and all of your behaviors. If people don't like you or don't find you attractive, there's a reason for it. If you are willing to look at whatever that reason is and make some changes, there is something you can do about it.

Studies performed by Dr. William Menniger indicate that the majority of people who are fired don't lose their jobs because of a lack of technical skills, but rather because of a lack of interpersonal skills. They can't get along with someone with whom they work. He states, "Their inability to get along with others accounts for 60 to 80 percent of the failures. Only 20 to 40 percent are fired due to incompetence."

Studies at the Carnegie Institute of Technology conclude that approximately 15 percent of a person's financial success is due to his technical knowledge and the other 85 percent is due to his ability to get along with and lead other people.

Both of these studies indicate that if we are to be successful, we need to be likable.

How would you describe your personality? Warm? Responsive? Cold? Standoffish? Edgy? Prickly? Sarcastic? How would someone else describe you? Do people have to watch what they say around you? Do you have such strong opinions that you won't listen or try to understand the other person's point of view? Do you have a chip on your shoulder? Do you take offense easily? Is it possible you could be wrong? Be assured it is not pleasant for others to be around someone who has to be right all the time. Nor is it pleasant to be around people who won't listen to what others have to say. If you want to develop a personality that will be attractive to others and have new acquaintances who want to get to know you better, then don't state your opinion as though it is an edict from above.

Learn to say, *You could be right. I've always looked at it from this position* . . . and then state your side of the discussion. The majority of subjects most people argue about are trivial matters. Keep in mind the other person may have some information or knowledge about the matter that you don't have.

Discuss controversial subjects only when you know the listeners are free of any bias. It is a total waste of your time to try to convince someone with a closed mind that he is wrong and it often makes an enemy of him.

Don't use yourself as an example of how others should be. This doesn't mean you shouldn't take credit for things you do well. It means not to lessen the self-esteem of others by pointing out their weakness and insecurities or comparing them to your strengths.

Don't express your opinions as opinion. Either convey your opinions as statements or don't say them at all. If you don't have the knowledge that enables you to put forth an informed statement, then you are better off keeping your mouth shut and your opinions to yourself.

Don't flatter or praise people when they don't deserve it. This is known as "buttering up" other people and makes them leery of you. It tears down trust in a relationship. They begin to suspect that you want something from them.

Never say you will or won't do something unless you are definite about whether or not you will do it. When you mean yes or no, don't say "maybe" or you will "try." And don't express favor of or opposition to anything unless you can say it in a positive manner with sincerity and reason.

When you show respect to others, you build your power and likeability factor at the same time. Think of the people you enjoy being around. They allow you to be yourself without compromising their own individuality.

Your disposition is your responsibility

You weren't born with the personality you have today. You developed it.

Some people seem to think theirs is genetic or hereditary. People often say to me, *You must have a really bad temper, because you have red hair.* If I did have a bad temper, which I don't, I'm sure it wouldn't be because of the color of my hair.

Disposition is a carry-over from childhood. Maybe you had a bad childhood. How long are you going to let your past use up today and the rest of your life? How long are you going to be immature? As a child, you were a victim of what happened to you. If you carry that over into your adulthood, then you become a volunteer victim of your past. You must take responsibility for you, your actions, your behaviors, your successes, or your failures. No one else in this world is going to take responsibility for you. They may want to take credit for the good things you do or the things at which you excel, but you are the only one responsible for you and that includes your personality. It's not a permanent part of you like the color of your eyes or the color of your skin. It is something you can develop, cultivate, and improve. It is the way you present yourself to the world.

Charisma

There is a mystical aspect to a charismatic personality. People recognize it and respond to it, but often don't know how to get it. Your charisma develops as you learn to accept people for their abilities, talents, skills, attitudes, and opinions without making judgments. If you will consider the other person's feelings and viewpoints, you will project warmth and understanding. Show interest in people. Always remind yourself that they are as proud, ambitious, and sensitive as you are. How would you feel if you were in their place? We never know what others have been through to get where they are today. They are probably doing the best they can. Because of their nationality, race, culture, religion, position in the organization, or any number of other factors, they are different than us. Good! How boring the world would be if everyone were just like us! Show an interest in the difference. Make an effort to learn something from every person you meet. Prejudice is a tell-tale sign of an ignorant person. It is also an outward expression of our fear of the unknown. That which we don't understand, we either dismiss as unnecessary, or fear as threatening.

Do you know how you sound?

As a child, when I would misbehave, my mother would quote an Irish poem by Robert Burns:

> *O would some Power gift to give us,*
>
> *To see ourselves as others see us*
>
> *It would from many a blunder free us.*

I often thought it might be even more revealing, "to hear ourselves as others hear us." Most of us own mirrors. We can look at ourselves now and then, but how many of us really know what we sound like, especially when we are engaged in conversation with others?

When we first attract the attention of others, they subconsciously anticipate what we will sound like when we speak. If the first sound out of our mouths is inferior to what they anticipate, they will assume we will not be what they expected either.

If our voice is superior to what they anticipated and is pleasing to their ears as well as their hearts, they will instantaneously like and trust us.

In the quest for power, the one attribute most often neglected is the voice. A great voice is engaging. Dr. Albert Mehrabian, a professor at UCLA who spent more than 20 years researching the communication process, tells us the sound of a person's voice accounts for 38 percent of one's ability to convey a message when engaged in one-on-one communication situations. Yet most people don't do anything to make sure their speaking voice is both pleasant and powerful. If you have a voice that is shrill, sharp, harsh, whiny, too high, too low, or sounds like baby talk, you may be turning people off before they even hear what you have to say. They will discount your information even before taking the time to digest it.

A clear, pleasant-sounding voice will entice people to listen to you and respond in a positive manner. When you have a warm, well-modulated voice you will be perceived for your substance. Your voice plays a significant part in your ability to convince and influence others.

Recently, I attended a speaker's association meeting. When the attendees introduced themselves, one of them announced she was a speech coach. This woman had a high, squeaky, unpleasant, little girl voice. How many people do you think rushed right out to hire her to teach them how to speak in public? Zero. Her own voice discounted her credibility. Regardless of the voice you were born with, you can do exercises and modulate your voice so it sounds soft and natural. It is essential to have a pleasant voice, especially in the world of business.

You don't want a voice that draws attention to you. You want a voice that people are not consciously aware of, a voice that is inviting, and one that gets people to listen to what you have to say because they have an interest in who you are. Most of us are greatly influenced by sound. That is why most newscasters and radio disc jockeys have such wonderful voices. These voices promote listening and that's what stations want . . . more listeners!

Most people with great voices were not born with them. They learned and practiced. Katie Couric trained her voice to be what it is today and look where it has taken her . . . anchoring the nightly news on a major television network!

Your voice represents your personality. It reveals your disposition, your mood, and your feelings. In ancient Greece, actors wore masks that covered a portion of their faces and amplified their voices. The part of the face that was covered — the bridge and sides of the nose down to and around the lips — became known as our "mask." When you project through this mask, it allows your voice, to become flexible, warm, and full of expression, giving your voice more range and more power.

There are six factors to be considered when determining voice quality: pitch, tone, volume, rate, control, and vocal variety.

Pitch

Most peoples' voices have two pitch levels: a correct or natural pitch level, and the one we normally use, which is known as the habitual pitch level. If these are not the same, we are misusing our voices.

Tone

In his book, *Change Your Voice, Change Your Life*, Morton Cooper suggests we imagine the throat as a megaphone that projects the voice, divided into three areas: the lower, middle and upper throat. The upper throat is the area behind the nose; the middle throat is the area behind the mouth; and the lower throat surrounds the larynx, or voice box. Resonance, or tone focus, should be produced from all three areas. Too much emphasis on any one area can create a misused voice. All excellent voices are projected from the upper two-thirds of the throat.

Be aware of emotions that sneak into your voice as you talk. How do you sound to others? Do you sound cranky? Tired? Bored? Hurried? Impatient? Catty? Angry? Disgusted? Your voice may reveal things about you that you will wish later you had kept to yourself.

Learn to express your more attractive moods, your best self, and your kind heart through your voice. Unpleasant expression of feelings, moods, and tempers don't exhibit control or power and have no place in cohesive relationships. Your speaking voice and the persona it expresses by its warmth or coolness will influence how people react to you and help make you either a success or a failure.

Volume

Be sure to speak at the appropriate volume . . . neither too loud nor too soft. You must speak just loud enough to be heard by others without them having to strain to hear you, and yet not so loud that people feel you are being aggressive or pushy. I have a friend who often visits from another country. She's fascinated with Americans and the things we do. During one of our trips, we were on an airplane when she turned to me and asked, "Why do Americans tell their personal business to total strangers and talk so loud that people four rows away from them also hear about it?" I didn't have an answer, but I have noticed it as well. Many of us don't know how to speak at a volume appropriate to the situation, and while some may be hard of hearing, many just don't have consideration for others.

Pacing

As a rule, women have a tendency to speak higher and faster than men. This is one of the reasons men think women are more "emotional" than they are. A lower-pitched, slower-paced voice will give you more credibility.

The rate of speed at which you speak should be a natural conversational pace. Many voice experts agree we should speak at a rate of approximately 126 words per minute. This gives the listener time to understand your meaning. If you articulate your words, it will assist in the reduction of speed. Most careless speech is a result of speaking too quickly. Also, if you slow up, you will tone down your voice.

Fast talking sometimes gets on people's nerves and irritates them. Because of our current hurry up and get everything done "urgency addiction," many people talk at a rate of 150 words per minute with gusts up to 200 words per minute. Speaking too rapidly could make your listeners believe you are insecure and afraid they will not listen to you, so you talk fast to be sure you get everything in before they leave. Speaking rapidly, especially if you don't take a breath between sentences or thoughts, will definitely not make people want to listen to you, but instead, will make them want to get away from you quickly.

When you speak too slowly, you can become boring and lose your listener. A person can listen at a rate of approximately 800 words per minute, so if you are talking at a pace of 60 or 80 words per minute, the listener's mind will go somewhere else and have its own conversation.

Breath control

Put one hand on your chest and the other on the area where your chest and your stomach meet. This is your diaphragm. Now, take a deep breath. If your chest and shoulders rise as you take in breath, you are breathing incorrectly. When you breathe in, you should feel your stomach come forward. This tells you the breath is in the proper place to fully support your voice. Upper chest breathing creates tension and strains the voice, while breathing from the diaphragm supports your voice and gives it a richer, more resonant tone.

Variety

Many women are uncomfortable in positions of responsibility and speak in tentative tones. Your voice is your instrument to deliver your thoughts, feelings, and knowledge. It is capable of great variety. Listen to radio personalities speak and note how they change their tone in order to give vocal variety and keep you interested in what they have to say. They don't have sing-song voices. They have strong, clear voices.

If you feel strongly or are excited about something, you will usually speak with interest, inflection, and excitement in your voice. If you speak with warm inflection at all times, you put yourself across to others as being interesting, fascinating, and definitely out of the ordinary. It takes energy to speak with vitality and emphasis. By cultivating this high energy vitality in your voice, stressing words and syllables that make your meaning clear, you indicate your strength of feeling and the importance of the information you are imparting.

Rising inflection

When we make a statement with a rising inflection at the end of the sentence, it sounds as though we are asking a question or seeking approval. This could indicate subordination and uncertainty. Be sure to speak your statements of fact with a downward inflection.

Get yourself a tape recorder and record yourself when you are having normal conversations with others or when you are on the telephone. Play the tape back and listen to your own voice. You will soon discover which areas need work.

Tell them who you are

There's no question about it; what you say and how you say it will reveal who you believe you are. It's imperative for you to keep your emotions under control when conversing with others. Be sure you are showing the emotion you want to show at the time and place you want to show it. Your attitude strongly influences the quality of your voice and your ability to communicate effectively. Make sure your entire demeanor is saying what you mean.

Power belongs to those who shed their insecurities and react to life in an active and positive manner.

Say What You Mean Exercise

Write down the names of seven people who have made a difference in your life. Write every positive feeling you have about them and your relationship with them. Take the time to write clear, concise sentences that convey your meaning and your feeling. Once you have completed this task and are satisfied with what you have written, make copies and send one to each of them.

The more you develop your skill at clear thinking and writing, the easier it will become to communicate verbally as well.

1. _____

   _____

   _____

   _____

2. _____

   _____

   _____

   _____

3. _____

   _____

   _____

   _____

4. _____

   _____

   _____

5. _____

6. _____

7. _____

Communication Affirmation

My thoughts and feelings are valid. I listen with interest. I share openly and honestly. I communicate my ideas with confidence and clarity. I become a better communicator every day, which brings me closer to the fulfillment of my goals. I say what I mean and sound like I mean it. I am more than enough.

Chapter Nine

Establish Your Look

Style is being yourself, on purpose.

— RAQUEL WELCH, ACTRESS

ithout even saying a word, you are transmitting a message with your appearance. Your physical presence is the foundation upon which you build your credibility. Analyze and thoughtfully plan how you will present yourself. Is your style on *purpose* . . . your purpose? Is the message your appearance gives the message you want people to receive? Do you project an attitude of success?

While attending a professional women's meeting recently with one of my executive friends, I observed the two women running the meeting had appearances that in no way indicated they were high-powered. They both wore pink jersey knit tops and neither of them wore jackets. Their bras were obviously not the correct undergarments to wear under such thin, knit jersey tops, because their breasts were not properly supported. Both women's breasts jiggled when they walked. Their nipples were standing out like headlights and one woman's nipples were even at different levels by a couple of inches. These two women stood there, side by side, speaking with enthusiasm about their new organization, but I'm sure no one heard a word either of them said! It was impossible to concentrate on what they were saying, because their physical appearances were so distracting. There was one man in the group and he seemed to be trying to figure out where to look . . . or rather, where **not** to look.

We make judgments about others based on their appearance. In fact, in the first seven seconds of meeting someone, we make judgments about his or her economic level, educational level, trustworthiness, social position, level of sophistication, level of success, moral character, and even social and educational heritages. How many times have you heard people say, "They come from old money," or "They're *nouveau riche* (new money)." I doubt many people are even aware of how closely they scrutinize others. However, there is probably not much they miss.

Just the other day, I caught myself making a judgment about the escrow officer who was helping me when I was signing some legal documents. She had shaved off her eyebrows and drawn new ones from the bridge of her nose straight up to her hairline, giving her the appearance of a devil or a Klingon from *Star Trek*! I was sitting there thinking, "She couldn't be very smart if she'd do that to her own face. I wonder if she knows how that looks?" Then I realized I wasn't concentrating on the business at hand. Do other people do this as well? You bet they do. That's why we don't want our appearances to detract from the situation or keep people from hearing what we have to say.

Nonverbal communication

When you see a person from a distance, the first thing you will see is the person's silhouette. This tells more about the person than most people even imagine. Her overall posture, how she stands, and how she positions her body tells others who she believes herself to be.

You can spot winners or losers 20 feet away. Their posture clearly indicates how they feel about themselves, and their confidence level.

In *The Magic of Believing*, Claude M. Bristol states, "The very way you walk, the way you carry yourself, your talk, your manner of dress, all reflect your way of thinking. A slovenly carriage is an indication of slovenly thinking, whereas an alert, upright carriage is the outward sign of inward strength and confidence. What you exhibit outwardly, you are inwardly. You are the product of your own thought. What you believe yourself to be, you are."

The nonverbal messages you send come from two sources: body language and image. To get your message across and make a favorable impression, you must demonstrate what you mean with purposeful movement and appropriate nonverbal communication. Dr. Albert Mehrabian's research, referred to in the previous chapter, also tells us that 55 percent of our ability to get our message across to others comes from our nonverbal communication — what others see about us.

To some of you, the following information is going to seem very basic. Even though some of us know these things, we occasionally fall into bad habits unless they are brought to our attention. Be conscious of this information and always remember to keep it in mind.

Body language

Although body language is the first language we all learned, most of us aren't conscious of it on a daily basis. Our body language is made up of our physical characteristics, facial expressions, posture, and mannerisms. It is reflexive and often involuntary language. I have heard, "it is more difficult to lie with our body language than with our speech." We can learn to use our body language effectively. Mannerisms like nailbiting, lip-chewing, hair-twisting, and leg-jiggling say you aren't confident. Dangling your shoe is also distracting and appears as though you are trying to be seductive.

Powerful people don't fidget. Their body language is slow, controlled, and purposeful. They know how to send effective non-verbal messages to those with whom they come in contact.

Visual poise

Body language falls into a category known as ***visual poise***. Visual means "that which we see." The word poise means "in balance." If we are going to make a powerful impression on others, we need everything they see about us to be in balance.

Body position and posture

Powerful people don't slump. They stand up straight. Good body posture makes you look confident, successful and energetic. There are many benefits to good body posture, including increased energy, improved health by aligning internal organs, and enhanced voice quality. In addition, you will look and feel more fit and self-assured.

Ask someone to look at your posture and see if you are standing correctly. A side view of your body should appear as though it has an invisible line starting at the crown of the head, flowing through the lobe of the ear, the outermost top of the shoulder, the hipbone, the center of the knee, and ending at the arches of the feet.

Good posture is a reflection of good health and high self-esteem. If you take care of your body, exercise, stand and sit up straight, you'll feel better about yourself and demonstrate that feeling to others. This gives them more confidence in you.

Walking with purpose

Walk as if you are going somewhere important. Put some energy into your step. Move purposefully.

The length of your step should be the same as the length of one of your feet. If you take longer steps, this will cause your hips to swing from side to side. If your steps are too short, it will give you the appearance of a wind-up doll.

Slightly overlap one foot in front of the other as you walk, making the transference of weight from foot to foot even and soundless. You don't want to have a loud, distinguishable walk where people say, "Here comes Sally!" before they can even see you.

Keep your knees eased and relaxed when walking. Don't lock your knees, as it will cause the body to have jerky motions. Allow your arms to swing naturally from the shoulder, keeping them close to the body with the palms of your hands turned inward. Don't bend them at the elbows when you walk or you might be mistaken for a member of the local drill team!

Keep your shoulders back and your head held high. Always be aware of your posture and your outward appearance.

Appearing interested

Once you have made your initial appearance with your silhouette and your posture, don't forget good posture should be carried through to many other things you do in life besides walking and standing; for example, sitting. Other people observe the way we sit, especially in meetings. If you want to make a favorable impression, sit up in your chair and lean forward slightly, keeping your eyes focused on the person who is talking. This indicates you are interested in what he or she has to say.

Crossing your legs when sitting makes the legs look larger and can cut off the circulation in your top leg. This can cause your leg to fall asleep. If the circulation is cut off often enough and long enough, it can lead to, or aggravate, varicose veins.

When we are nervous, bored, or impatient and our legs are crossed, we will often swing the top leg back and forth. This calls attention to the leg and your state of mind, rather than keeping others focused on what you have to say. If you absolutely must sit with one leg crossed over the other leg, be sure to turn your body so that your legs are parallel to each other and pointed in the same direction. This doesn't cut off the circulation and will allow the blood to flow freely. Resist the urge to wrap your top foot around the bottom leg.

All in all, it's better to keep your feet side by side and your knees together.

Making an entrance

Whenever you enter a room, you want your entrance to be favorably noticed.

If you are too tentative, you may lose your audience before you get to open your mouth. If you run in looking harassed and frazzled and slide into the closest chair, you will also defeat yourself. Walk in confidently and with good posture. Project confidence — you have a reason to be there and something important to offer. Pause for a moment, look around the room and choose where you will sit. If the situation allows, introduce yourself to those around you. If you already know them, acknowledge them. Even if you are late, enter purposefully and simply say, "I apologize for the interruption. I was unavoidably delayed." This is powerful. Overexplaining, giving reasons, or making excuses is not powerful.

When you walk into a room where someone is working, pause until that person acknowledges your presence.

If a meeting is held in a room with theater-style seating, making it necessary for you to enter and exit rows where people are seated, turn your body to face the people who are seated. In this way, you will avoid stepping on people's feet, plus it will keep your backside out of their faces.

It also brings you face-to-face with the people, so you can speak to them and say, "Excuse me," as you pass, letting them know you are poised and confident.

Exiting a room

When leaving a meeting room full of people, turn to face those you are leaving before you step through the doorway. Then, step through at an angle, so the last view anyone has of you is a profile rather than your back side. Close doors quietly. Slamming a door, even when angry, is not effective and only serves to make you look childish.

Other tips

★ Stand up at the end of meetings.

★ Stand up when anyone enters or leaves your office.

★ Hold doors for handicapped persons, senior citizens, and people carrying packages.

★ Always thank anyone who holds a door open for you.

★ Give up your seat to anyone who appears older than you, frail, or pregnant.

Facial expressions

Your facial expressions let people know how you feel. A smile is the best way to demonstrate a cheerful attitude, approval, or enjoyment. In business, this is a great asset. A warm smile when you greet people, acknowledge people, or do business with people is always appropriate and usually welcomed. Granted, if you have problems or the situation is serious, your facial expression needs to be appropriate. It is possible, however, to have a serious expression and still look pleasant.

Your eyebrows sometimes say more about your thoughts than you mean to reveal. Raised eyebrows can indicate questioning, surprise, or even nervousness. Crinkled foreheads and knitted brows often indicate confusion, indecision, perplexity, or consternation. Scorn and ridicule usually come across when we arch our brows.

I have one friend who has had so many injections of Botox cosmetic, which temporarily paralyzes the facial muscles, she can't move her eyebrows or most of the rest of her face, for that matter. Our facial expressions give meaning to our words. Don't get so many of these shots that you can't make an expression! There are directors in Hollywood who won't hire actors or actresses who have had Botox injections, because they feel it inhibits an actor's ability to show emotions. Also, never cover your face with your hair so people can't see or read your expressions.

Eye contact

Your eyes are the focal point of your face. Use your eyes effectively to make eye contact and others will believe you to be confident and direct. The way you look at a person can make that person either comfortable or uncomfortable, so it is important to control where you look and how long you maintain eye contact. When you are trying to make an important point, it is imperative to look at the listener. Look at the person's entire face. This will give you a good indication of whether or not the person is interested in what you have to say. In the American business culture, we have a tendency to look others in the eye when we are comfortable or wanting to ensure trust. If you avoid eye contact, it may be interpreted as a sign of weakness, guilt, or low self-esteem. If you stare at the other person, it can be interpreted as a challenge. In order to avoid this, break eye contact briefly by glancing over that person's shoulder from time to time.

In many other cultures around the world, looking down is a means of showing respect and looking directly at a person is considered very rude. Be sure you are not misreading someone else's eye contact message because you are unfamiliar with his or her culture.

Nodding

Nodding shows the other person you are listening and understanding what is being said. It lets the other person know you are agreeing with her without interrupting her to verbally say you agree.

If you are in a group and want the speaker to notice you, nod. The speaker believes the person who is nodding is very smart to be in agreement and will speak straight to that person. Be careful not to overdo it to the point where you look like a bobble-head statue in the back window of someone's car.

Shaking Hands

Whether you are meeting someone for the first time or you're meeting a customer, client, or colleague you've known, pause to focus on the person you are greeting, look that person in the eye and smile as though you are genuinely glad to see him or her. Don't stand behind your desk when greeting someone. There should be nothing between you and the other person except space. Offer to shake hands. Extend your right hand toward the other person. Clasp palm to palm; be firm. Your handshake should display your sense of confidence, but not crush the other person's hand. This gesture is offered to anyone with whom you are doing business. It conveys certainty, confidence, and competence. If you offer a firm, friendly handshake, it is interpreted as "professionalism," but don't put your left hand over the other person's hand while shaking hands. This can be construed as a power play or one-upmanship. It is appropriate to shake hands at both the beginning and end of meetings.

A handshake is really the only physical contact you will have in a business encounter. Notice how people greet you, whether or not they offer their hands to shake, whether or not they enunciate their names clearly and distinctly and ask your name. Notice, too, whether or not they show a genuine interest in you. This will give you an immense amount of information. If the handshake you are given is brief and abrupt, offered with no eye contact, then it is likely the other person is not expecting the encounter to be successful. Historically, handshakes were used to show that no one was holding a weapon and a clasp on the forearm was how a person made sure the person he faced was not hiding a weapon up his sleeve. Today, it is a generally accepted worldwide business practice for both men and women to offer a handshake. It doesn't matter who offers first. It is believed the person who extends a hand first has an advantage. She is taking the initiative, being direct, and taking control of the situation. As many men find it awkward even today to offer their hand to a woman, smart women offer their hands first. If a man offers you his hand first, take it as a compliment. He is clearly telling you he is including you in the same business practices in which he includes men.

Hands

While we are on the subject of hands, please remember they are a part of your nonverbal message. Every time you shake someone's hand, sign a document, or lift an eating utensil, your hands tell the other person something about you.

If your hands are dry, chapped and cracked, it certainly won't feel good to the other person shaking your hand.

If you have chipped nail polish or broken or chewed nails, you may appear nervous, sloppy, and inattentive to details. If you have dirty nails or they appear dirty because you have stains from hair dye, ink, shoe polish, or furniture polish under the nail or around the cuticle, people will not want to shake hands with you.

Even worse are those long sculptured nails that are an inch beyond the end of the finger. What on earth do you imagine gets trapped under those? I'm not talking about the nicely manicured, sculptured nails that are well groomed. I'm talking about the ones that are very long. Some of them are so long they even start to curl under the fingers. Often nails this long have been broken and glued back together a few times and it shows. Some women have paintings, artwork, or decals on the nails, or pierced studs through the nail. These may be acceptable if you are a rock star, but they have no place in a business office, especially if you are dealing with people's money or handling food.

Nail polish can also be a detriment to your career. Colors like purple, black, green, or yellow should be reserved for a costume party and not worn at work. Matte cream polish in neutral shades of pink and peach are most appropriate for business. French manicures, or unpolished, buffed nails which are shaped well, are also attractive.

Elbows

Be sure to put lotion on your elbows regularly so they don't crack or dry out. When elbows get dry, they take on the appearance of being dirty. This little detail is one you don't want to overlook.

Talking with your hands

Family members often teased my sister about talking with her hands and she became quite self-conscious about it. Actually, if you use your hands a lot when you talk, you project yourself as an energized, enthusiastic person. Etiquette research has found that people who use their hands when they talk are more engaging than people who keep their hands in their pockets or out of sight in some other way. If you don't gesture with your hands freely, at least keep them where they can be seen. You will be considered by others to be more trustworthy.

Hair

Since your hair is near your face, it will get a lot of attention. Actually, hair is often the first thing one notices about another person. Be sure your hairstyle is complimentary to your face shape and gives a professional appearance. Any coloring done to your hair should be professionally done, or at the very least, should look as though it was professionally done. Color needs to appear as though it is your natural hair color. Be sure not to have hair of one color and roots of another or a color that is not a natural hair color — like blue or neon pink!

Teeth

As I travel the world, I am astounded at the lack of importance many people place on their teeth. Good grief. There are whole cultures of people out there with ugly mouths. Your teeth are a part of your smile. A great smile is a vital part of a professional demeanor. How are you going to have an effective, powerful smile, if you have yellow or brown teeth or worse yet, you have teeth missing in the front of your mouth? When people meet you, they instantly notice your teeth. If your teeth are bad, they immediately discount you as being ignorant or broke . . . or both.

Dental hygiene is essential for an attractive smile. You should brush your teeth a minimum of two times a day and floss as often. This will remove food particles and plaque and will keep your teeth and gums healthy. In addition, brushing and flossing helps prevent bad breath. Have your teeth professionally cleaned at least once a year.

Some of you are thinking, "Geez, Judi, I am not a child. I know to brush my teeth." I am sure you do! I'll also bet you know someone who has bad breath or teeth that could use a brushing or two. We have all encountered seemingly intelligent people working with the public who have ugly or rotten teeth and smelly breath. Some people are afraid of going to a dentist, yet those people should be aware there have been tremendous strides in dentistry in the past few years. Now you can get a fabulous smile without the pain, suffering, or expense it used to require. Between bonding, bleaching, and veneers, you can literally have a great new smile in a week!

My dentist showed me a video of one of his patients who is a card dealer at a local casino. This woman, who is in her 50's, had small, crooked, yellow teeth. The dentist fitted her for veneers and the final result was breathtaking. She looked sensational. The dentist told me since she has had her new teeth and bright smile, her tips at work have *doubled*! She appears to be friendlier and more fun, because she smiles more now and the customers enjoy playing at her table. Consequently, they tip her more. Do you still think a winning smile doesn't make a great impression? What does your smile say about you?

Keep some breath mints handy. Under no circumstances should you ever chew gum in the workplace as you will be perceived as unprofessional. Actually, it's not in good taste to chew gum in public — ever!

Practice your visual poise techniques daily and they will become second nature to you. Even if you should make a mistake, recovery will be easy.

Image and dress

Your image and the way you dress speak louder and more eloquently about you than anything you actually say. Clothing plays a vital role in how others see you. How others see you plays a vital role in your career advancement or lack of it. You will probably never get a career advancement because of your wardrobe, but your wardrobe choices may hold you back. It's a lot harder to advance if your wardrobe is contributing to the projection of an incorrect image.

Many women today are confused about what is proper business attire and which attire will take them to the top of the corporate ladder or get the account they have been chasing. It's no wonder they are confused. Very few companies have dress codes, so there really are no rules as to the ideal way to dress for business. Women have never had a traditional style of dressing compared to the man's business suit. Many companies have adopted casual days or casual dress codes which have resulted in 55 percent of employees dressing down daily for work and 90 percent wearing casual clothing at least one day a week. It doesn't help that movies and television show business women wearing skimpy tops and mini-skirts or skin-tight dresses and pants.

Brooke, who is 19, came down for breakfast dressed for her office job in a camisole top and hip-hugger, skin-tight pants that showed her belly button and her belly button jewelry. Her mother asked, "Are you planning to wear that to work? It's really not appropriate." Brooke's reply was, "Well, it was on display in the department store and Britney Spears dresses this way." Her mom explained to her that Britney does not work in a law office. Brooke changed, but she was very upset.

The department stores and the fashion industry don't care if you are successful or not. They want you to buy clothes. Clothing that looks great on a 5'9" stick-thin model doesn't often look good on a shorter person with real curves to her body.

Business attire should convey a look and feeling of presence, authority, and trust. The younger you are, the more conservative the clothing needs to be to achieve this effect.

Megan told her mother she was going to get her neck tattooed. Her mom begged her not to do it. She said, "But Mom, I work in a boutique and I need to look funky." Her mother tried to explain that she probably wouldn't work in a boutique forever, and while that tattoo may be wonderful right now, it would be permanent. At 35, she might not feel the same way about the tattoo and many companies don't hire people with tattooed necks. Megan was upset and felt this was unfair; people should hire her for her ability, not for how she looks or dresses. We can all understand that may be the way it should be, but the reality is that it's not the way it is. Studies conducted by economists at the University of Texas at Austin and Michigan State University found people who are perceived as good looking and attractive earn higher incomes than those who are not. Additionally, women who wear makeup earn more than women who don't. Acceptable makeup for business means attractive, natural looking makeup, not heavy caked-on Las Vegas showgirl stage makeup or black Gothic lipstick.

Consider your career goal every time you dress for work. Consider, too, what the leaders in your industry wear. Then combine your own personal style with a sense of what is appropriate in your place of business and for the next level to which you aspire in your career. Always have the appearance of someone who would be in the next higher position. People who look the part often get promoted over someone who may have more ability but not look the part. It may not be fair but those are the facts. Be sure you have *both* the ability and the look. It's smart to dress in a manner that will help you get to the next level rather than hold you back.

Virtually every industry has its own unwritten clothing code. Conservative fields such as law, banking and insurance still demand a rather subdued dress style. Suits will dominate the wardrobes of professionals in these fields. You can, however, personalize your style with the cut, the fabric, the colors, and the accessories. Other types of businesses, such as advertising, cosmetics, retailing, film, or television demand a more dramatic look. You'll want to convey more flair and show you are on the cutting edge of what's new, while still managing to maintain a professional appearance. Many occupations demand that you have the ability to be like a chameleon, changing your look to fit the environment of the day. While I do prescribe that businesswomen maintain a simple tailored, conservative look, you don't have to look like a little grey mouse that blends in with the woodwork. Your look should convey confidence, originality, and professional success.

While many companies have instituted a casual dress day once a week, usually Friday, there are very few, if any, guidelines for what casual dressing means. On a recent Friday, I had appointments at three different companies and at each appointment, the executive I met with apologized to me for her dress and then added that it was "casual Friday." Why on earth would you wear something to work that you feel needs an explanation or an apology? This casual dress undoubtedly made these three people feel as though they weren't dressed appropriately for our meetings and would not be perceived as effective, competent, and professional in their positions. Guess what? They were right. I took the time and care to dress myself appropriately for a business meeting and by doing so, placed myself in a power position above the person with whom I was meeting. Not because they were not capable, but simply because they were not dressed and presented properly.

Business casual means a nice skirt or slacks and a jacket or blazer that can be slipped on over a casual, tailored blouse for client meetings. Jeans, jogging suits, sweatsuits, lowrider and hiphugger slacks, t-shirts with sayings or logos other than company logos, underwear worn as outerwear, such as chemise tops, camisoles and tank tops, don't belong in an office even on casual day. If you would wear it to the beach, to work in the garden, on a date, or even out bumming around with friends, don't wear it to work.

Put a little more thought and a bit more strategizing into your wardrobe. Think about what you want to achieve by what you are wearing.

Image as a tool

Clothing is one way a person evaluates another. If we are careless about our attention to our clothing, others intuitively pick up unintended and potentially confusing messages from our physical presence.

Dressing ourselves is an invaluable tool to communicate who we are and our intention, whether it is authority, professionalism, friendliness, gentleness, or warmth. It is impossible to "not communicate."

If we are overlooked in a crowded room, we are visually conveying to others either that we wish to fade into the background or we are unapproachable. As I have had a challenge with my weight most of my life, I would sometimes try not to be noticed. When I was going through one of my larger clothing size experiences, I was telling a friend of mine how unhappy I was with the way I looked in my clothing. She gave me a marvelous piece of advice. She said, "Honey, if you can't hide it, decorate it. If we are attractive, well-groomed and charming, people don't sit around wondering how much we weigh." I've been decorating it ever since!

When we receive unwanted sexual advances, we could be communicating an unintended message. If this is happening to you, hire an image consultant to assess your body language and assist you with selecting a more powerful wardrobe. In addition, learn to be more assertive in your verbal communication. We are each responsible for the way others respond to us.

Our visual presence always talks and is one of the most overlooked but significant expressions of our personal power and uniqueness.

Selecting your wardrobe

Quality shows . . . in people and in clothes. It is important to your career for you to consider purchasing quality clothing. People who know the difference will recognize that you know the difference, too. It is better to have fewer pieces of well-made, quality clothing than lots of clothing that is poorly made or too trendy.

Solid colors are the wisest choices for your wardrobe. A high quality suit in navy, grey, black, or taupe will be appropriate for almost any professional occasion and can be easily accessorized. Add drama and flair with brightly colored accessories. Watch the powers in your industry. See what the leaders wear to help you determine what is appropriate for where you are now and where you want to go.

Consider the fabric as well as the style and color when choosing items for your wardrobe. You don't want to buy clothing that wrinkles easily. Test the fabric by squeezing the material in one hand. When you let go, check to see if it is wrinkled. If it is, it will rapidly wrinkle when you wear it, so it's not a good choice.

Cost per wearing

Consider the cost-per-wearing formula. If you buy a classic cashmere suit for $675, rather than an inexpensive suit for $75, you will love that cashmere suit, feel like a million dollars in it and wear it more than the less expensive suit. If you wear the cashmere suit ten times a month for seven months, you will have worn it 70 times, which equals $9.64 per wearing. If you wear the inexpensive suit four times and it wrinkles every time you wear it, you won't feel very good in it and you will quit wearing it. That's $18.75 per wearing. So basically, the inexpensive suit costs you twice as much per wearing as the more expensive one, plus you won't even enjoy wearing it. On the other hand, the good cashmere suit is a classic style you can easily wear for four years. The cost per wearing now comes down to $2.41. If you will use this formula when purchasing your career clothing, you will have a more powerful wardrobe and spend less money in the long run.

Basic wardrobe list

The following wardrobe will enable you to go anywhere in the world for two weeks and be appropriately dressed at all times:

Two   Suits that can be worn through three seasons
       (fall, winter, spring)

One   Summer suit

Three White or cream blouses (silk, linen, or fine cotton)

Three Summer-weight tailored dresses

One   Tailored dress in your basic color

Two   Sets of separates

One   Winter coat in your basic color

One   Trenchcoat with zip out lining in your basic color or beige

One   Leather handbag in your basic color

Two   Pair leather shoes in your basic color
       (one low heel; one high heel)

One   Pair earrings (gold, silver, or pearl)

One   Necklace – powerful, chunky (gold, silver, or pearl)

Remember, basic doesn't mean boring. With proper accessories, you can create a stunning look. To get ideas on accessorizing your wardrobe, look at fashion magazines or store displays. But don't buy anything unless you can answer these three questions positively:

(1) Do I have anything to wear with it? (2) Does it go with anything else? (3) Does it suit me? If your answer is anything other than "yes," then save your money.

Shoes are a must

You need to have shoes. They will probably be the most expensive of your accessories. They should fit well and be the best you can afford.

Select your shoes for practical use, as well as fashion mileage, or you will be sorry later. Flip-flops, hiking boots, stiletto heels and scruffy tennis shoes have a purpose in your wardrobe, but not in an office. If you must wear open-toe shoes and your company allows it, make sure you have a regular pedicure, even if you have to do it yourself. If you wear shoes with an open heel, make sure your feet are clean and moisturized. Dry, cracked, or callused heels are incredibly unattractive and could tell other people that you don't pay attention to details.

The classic pump is the best shoe for most business environments. Leather is the most practical type of shoe for work, as it is a natural material and allows your feet to breathe. It is also easier to maintain than cloth, suede, plastic, or patent leather. The best way to remember what time of year to wear which colors of shoes is to remember that your shoes should never be lighter in color than the color of the hemline on your skirt or pants. A black dress with white shoes screams, "I don't know how to dress myself!" White shoes are worn with white clothing only. Your best bet for a professional image is to choose shoe colors from the basic color range which includes navy, black, cordovan, and taupe.

Hosiery

If you work in a very conservative environment, wear hosiery that is skin toned. Colored hosiery should be worn only with the same color clothing, such as black nylons with black dresses or skirts or navy nylons with navy clothing. Never wear dark hosiery when you are wearing light-colored clothing or shoes.

Take a look at the hosiery of the top women executives in your field. That will give you an idea of what is acceptable in your industry. Remember, it is always better to err on the conservative side and be overly cautious than not cautious enough.

Jewelry

Your most important business accessory is your watch. Most of us wear a watch every day. Usually we wear the same one for business and for social functions, making it important to wear a watch that is classic in style as well as functional.

Earrings should be simple, yet elegant. As your earrings are near your face, you don't want them to be so flashy they attract people's attention to your earrings and away from what you are saying. Chandelier-style and dangling earrings produce movement and definitely attract attention. This may be what you want for a social scene, but not for your business meetings or in the office.

A rope chain of considerable size or a necklace with a focal point can be very effectively worn under an open collar blouse to give a subliminal message of power. Thin chains and feminine pendants will not give the same message.

Broaches or pins at the neckline, lapel, or on the shoulder all draw the eye toward the face which is what you want.

Bangles and charm bracelets should not be worn to the office as they make noise when you move your arm and can be very distracting to those around you. Anything that takes attention away from what you are saying and the message you want to convey should not be worn.

People often ask me, "How much jewelry should I wear?" or "How much jewelry is too much?" There's an easy rule to follow. It is called the "14 Point Accessorizing Method." Any eye-catching feature is considered a point. To be well-accessorized, you should wear fewer than 14 points. This will give you an understated, uncluttered appearance. Here's how you count the points; give yourself one point for each of the following:

★ Each color in your outfit.

★ Plain, simple shoes. Add an additional point for any details on shoes like open-toes, open-heels, bows, large buckles, chains, ropes or multi-colors.

★ Stockings that are any color other than skin tone.

★ Watches, chains, bracelets, a pair of earrings. If they are multi-colored, have stones, dangle or make noise, add a point for each one.

★ Glasses. Ornate glasses are two points.

- ★ Handbags: if tailored. If decorated with chains, buckles and extra colors, add one point for each color, chain, or charm.

- ★ Nail polish; toenail polish that is revealed is another point.

- ★ Buttons of a contrasting color to the garment.

- ★ Decoration such as bows, ruffles, contrasting belts, and scarves.

- ★ Red or platinum hair.

- ★ Don't add any points for engagement or wedding rings.

If your items add up to less than 14 points, you may be assured you are accessorized adequately. If you have 14 or more points, take off some of your accessories. Less is always more.

Glasses

If you need glasses, wear them. Squinting is not attractive and often gives your face an unpleasant look.

Glasses need to be attractive as well as functional. They should contribute positively to your image and enhance your facial features. If you can afford it, have more than one pair. Get a pair of glasses for work and something more casual for your personal life.

Handbags/briefcases/portfolios

Handbags and briefcases can be quite expensive. When made of high quality leather, they should last you through many seasons. Stay away from trendy looks for handbags, briefcases, and portfolios. A great purse or briefcase should look expensive. Choose a classic style in leather and as with shoes, stay with colors like navy, black, taupe, or cordovan.

Don't overload these items to the point where it looks like you have everything inside, including the kitchen sink. Scratching around in your purse to find business cards, keys, or a pen gives the appearance of being unorganized. It is perfectly acceptable to carry a handbag along with a briefcase or a portfolio, as long as they both contain only the necessary items needed for the day or the event. If you are carrying both, be sure the handbag is a shoulder bag that has a tailored appearance.

The pen you carry

The pen you carry should look expensive and be in good shape. You can ruin a good image when you ask a client to sign a contract with a cheap or chewed-up pen!

Overall plan for developing good taste

We can best define good taste as a conservative, refined look. Women with taste don't wear clothing that is offensive, unsuitable for their age or cluttered with complicated lines and details. These women make subtle adjustments to their basic wardrobes to be in fashion, but don't let the fashion world dictate what they wear. They don't wear a lot of inexpensive accessories, but rather, one or two pieces of real jewelry.

Freshness

Women of taste have an appearance of freshness. This does not mean acting "fresh." It means they appear neat, clean, and immaculately groomed. One company hired me to present an image program for their administrative personnel, because one woman was a mess. She was a senior member of the team and looked more like an unmade bed than a professional. Her hair was over-processed and brittle, resembling a haystack. Her clothing was not only too brief for her body and her age, it often had spots and stains. Her appearance did not reflect positively on the status of her position in the company.

People judge us by our grooming

Even the most expensive and best-fitting clothes won't overcome a bad image, if you haven't cared for them properly. Make sure your clothing is clean and pressed. Keep a lint brush in your desk or car so you can remove any lint your clothing may pick up during the day. Polish your shoes regularly and make sure they are in good repair with no worn-out heels or soles. When your shoes need new heel tips, take them to the shoe repair immediately.

Even if you bathe every day, your clothing will smell of body odor if you don't have them cleaned regularly. One very prominent professional woman I sat by at a meeting recently smelled so strongly of body odor, I nearly gagged. This was not a one-time occurrence. Other people had mentioned they couldn't stand to sit near her, because she smelled so bad. It's a shame, too, because this is a highly intelligent woman who has a lot to contribute to an organization, but she doesn't get the chance because of bad grooming habits. She probably doesn't even know the real reason people avoid her. Maybe she doesn't even know she is being avoided. Now that's detrimental to her goals.

A little perfume goes a long way

It's nice to have a clean, fragrant freshness about yourself, but when you smell like you bathed in perfume, it can be too much, especially for business. Some people have allergies to fragrances and will sneeze or get a sore throat from being around you if you are wearing too much. Others won't be able to tolerate the sweetness or strength of the smell. They may attempt to get away from you without ever telling you why.

I was on an airplane recently where one of the flight attendants had on so much perfume that every time she came whizzing by I had to hold my breath. On an airplane, there is no escape route.

Attractiveness is an attitude

Research by John T. Molloy, best known for his book, *Dress for Success*, tells us that attractive women are 20 percent more likely to be hired by another woman and 300 percent more likely to be hired by a man than unattractive women. Anyone can be attractive, so make it a point to be your most attractive self at all times. There is a fine line here to be considered though. Don't flaunt your good looks. People will resent your good looks if you are also arrogant and self-centered. You must portray caring, humility, and trustworthiness. You must also be capable of handling the responsibilities of your job, so others don't think you traded on your good looks to get where you are.

Many traits and behaviors make us more attractive to others ... smiling, good posture, good manners, dressing appropriately, a pleasant-speaking voice, graceful movements, and intelligence. You can establish any look you desire by determining your objective, making a plan, and visualizing the "you" that you want others to see. Act "as if" you already are the person you want to become and present yourself with style and purpose.

Establish Your Look Exercise

Go through your closet. Give away everything you haven't worn in the last year and everything you don't like or don't feel good wearing. If you haven't worn something in a year or you don't like something, you aren't going to start wearing it or liking it now.

Take out everything that doesn't fit right now. Give the items away. What good is it to stand and look at a closet full of clothes and say, "I don't have a thing to wear." Besides, you need to get yourself to your ideal size and stay there.

Buy some red hangers the next time you are at a discount department store. Then, hang any items that need repair on your red hangers and put them at one end of the closet until you get each item fixed. The red hangers will alert you not to wear the article again until it is repaired. You don't have to fix them yourself. Many dry cleaners have alterations experts who can put in a new zipper, stitch in a hem, or change buttons on a garment. The fee is minimal and your clothing item gets back into your working wardrobe much sooner than if you wait until you can get around to doing it.

Now, categorize and hang the clothing that is left in the closet into groups. Put suits together, blouses together, pants together, dresses together, etcetera. Hang each category by color from the dressiest to the sportiest.

Make a list of what you have. Most likely you will have more of one or two colors than anything else. Hopefully, the clothing color you have the most of will be one of the basic colors: black, brown, camel, navy, cordovan, taupe, or grey.

Compare what you have on your list with the basic wardrobe list in this chapter. After comparing your list to the Basic Wardrobe list, make yourself a shopping list. Anything that is on the basic wardrobe list that is not in your closet should go on your shopping list. Don't buy anything else until you get these items and your basic wardrobe is complete. No more impulsive buying. Buy the things you need in the order of importance to you and as your budget allows.

Shopping List

1. _____

   _____

2. _____

   _____

3. _____

   _____

4. _____

   _____

5. _____

   _____

6. _____

   _____

7. _____

   _____

Establish Your Look Affirmation

I present myself as I want to be seen. My clothes, my accessories, my grooming, and my attitude express the person I choose to be. I feel good because I look good. I look the part, act the part, and live up to my image of success. My style is on purpose . . . my purpose. I am more than enough.

Chapter Ten

Associate for Success

Keep away from people who try to belittle your ambitions. Small people always do that, but the really great make you feel that you, too, can become great.

— **MARK TWAIN**, AMERICAN HUMORIST AND WRITER

Who are your friends? Who are your associates? With whom do you spend the most time?

We don't always get to pick our relatives, but we can certainly choose who we seek out for friendship. Many of us haven't chosen our friends; we've just acquired them — through work, school, or associations. In many instances, negative people have somehow infiltrated themselves into our social circle. It is of uppermost importance to associate with positive people.

We learn our behaviors, habits, mannerisms, speech patterns, verbiage, and manners (or lack of them) from the people with whom we spend the most time. We pick up habits and ideas from the people with whom we associate. People who succeed put themselves in the company of other people who are striving to succeed. People who fail often hang around with people who have no goals and no ambition.

Success breeds success

If you associate with successful people, you will learn from them and you will be more likely to become successful, too. Successful people often present opportunities to people they know. The people with whom you associate should be people you can learn from, who are interesting, and have a positive outlook toward life. You should also be able to contribute something of value to their lives.

Make a list of the people with whom you usually associate. Then beside their names, write down their most outstanding characteristic. Whom would you like to emulate? Who is interesting? Who is negative or bad-mouths others? Who complains a lot? Who makes things happen? Which friends or associates are just getting by?

If you find there are negative people on your list, don't worry. You don't have to go right out and dump your friends. Think in terms of acquiring new friends and acquaintances who are positive and are headed where you want to go. When I wanted to become a speaker, I joined the National Speakers Association in order to associate with top notch speakers and learn from them. Later, I decided I wanted to write books as well, so I attended a writer's conference, and then joined a local writers' group. Because the people in these groups have similar interests to mine, we have commonalities and ways to help each other be successful.

Networking

I'm sure you've heard the phrase, "It's not what you know, it's who you know."

I believe it's both. Who you know can get you where you want to go. What you know keeps you there. I also believe it's who knows you . . . or at least knows who you are. Some of the most competent people I know have **not** made the effort to know people or be known by people who can help them get ahead. So their talents and abilities continue to get overlooked. If you want power and influence, associate with powerful, influential people and learn everything you can from them.

In his book, *Megatrends*, John Naisbitt reports that by networking, we can reach anyone in the world with only six person-by-person interactions. Networking is when we deliberately and consciously seek to make associations with people. It is not left up to chance.

In every organization, there are the leaders — people who have power and influence. Find out what groups they are involved in and attend group meetings. Get acquainted with them. Make sure to sit at their tables at events. Introduce yourself or get someone else to introduce you. Volunteer to be on their committee or task force.

The people you know can open doors and speed up your success. Make meeting new people a top priority and keep in touch with them regularly. You may want to choose a person who has achieved the same goals you would like to accomplish and ask that person to be your mentor. Don't be afraid to ask for help. Many times people are flattered if you point out that you are asking them because they are experts in their field and you would like to learn from them. Offer to assist them with a project or something they are doing. If you make it a habit to help others toward their goals, they usually are willing to help you as well.

In *The Secrets of Savvy Networking*, author Susan RoAne defines networking as "a reciprocal process, an exchange of ideas, leads, and suggestions that support both our professional and personal lives."

Be a community leader

If you want to be a community leader, join groups in which community leaders participate. Your local chamber of commerce, Soroptimists International, Rotary International, or Toastmasters International are good organizations to join. Get involved quickly. Volunteer to be on a committee or assist with registration. The very best opportunity to meet people is to be a greeter at functions. In this way, you are introducing yourself to everyone as they come in, because it is your job to welcome them to the meeting. When you are the greeter, it is your responsibility to make the other person feel comfortable. It keeps you from thinking about yourself and how uncomfortable you are when meeting new people — after you've done it a few times, you won't be uncomfortable anymore and you'll know everyone who attends the meetings regularly.

When you are attending a meeting, be sure to sit at a table with people you don't know. Doing so will afford you the opportunity to introduce yourself. One of the main benefits to belonging to these organizations and attending meetings is that you will be making contacts. You won't make contacts if you go with your friend and the two of you are so busy talking to each other that others won't speak to you for fear of interrupting. You won't make contacts if you don't introduce yourself to others and start conversations. If you introduce yourself to enough people, you will surely make some new positive, interesting friends in your field of business and acquire some good business contacts as well.

Pre-planning and preparation

Before attending any event, put some thought into why you are going there. Why are you attending this event? What is your primary goal and what do you hope to achieve? Would you like to make new contacts? If so, who and why? Do you plan on learning new information? Who might have that information? Are you trying to increase business? Will there be potential clients at this event? Are you trying to build your self-confidence as you meet new people or are you going just to have fun? Ask yourself these questions and then write out a statement of intent before going to the meeting. Include in this statement why you are going and what you intend to accomplish by going there.

Your statement might read like this: "By attending this event, I will introduce myself to a powerful and dynamic group of people who have the resources to use my product and/or services. It is my objective to hand out 25 business cards and return to my office with at least three qualified leads, as well as a definite commitment to telephone appointments with two people. I will do this in a manner that makes people want to see me and talk with me again. That manner is by showing an interest in them."

When you have a definite goal in mind, you will be better able to seek out those individuals you would like to meet and ask the questions you would like to ask. Because you are prepared, you will be amazed at the difference in what you will accomplish. Why would you spend all that time and money to go unprepared to an event and end up coming away without any benefits?

What to wear

Find out what the appropriate attire will be and clothe yourself accordingly. Then add an "extra" to be sure people remember you. Patricia Fripp, one of America's most exciting professional speakers, says, "There's no sense in going anywhere if people don't remember you've been there." Try to be memorable — by your appearance and by your conduct.

What time should you arrive?

Being on time is such a simple concept it's hard to imagine why so many people have difficulty getting where they said they would be at the time they said they would be there. With the pace of our lives today, time is of the essence. Having to wait on another person is frustrating and aggravating. Arriving late is rude. Habitually arriving late is downright disrespectful. If you want to be seen as a professional, it is imperative you learn to be on time. Busy people don't have much tolerance for needless waiting.

When you make an appointment with someone, make note of the time you need to leave your office or previous appointment, as well as the time you should arrive. Allow enough time for traffic delays or detours. Determine what time you need to leave and then leave at that time. Don't take one more phone call, do one more task, or stop to chat with one more person. Invariably these will make you late and being late is a broken commitment. You don't want to be perceived as a person who breaks commitments. This could ruin your reputation.

Cindy made it a habit to be late to events. She said if she was late, she could make a grand entrance and everyone would notice her. They noticed alright, but I don't believe anyone thought her "fashionably late entrance" was positive. In fact, in many cases, it was disruptive. She wanted to be the center of attention, but she didn't realize she was creating negative attention.

It is always in good taste to be on time. In fact, if you are not early, you're late. Getting to an event early gives you more time to meet new people, observe the room, and decide where you are going to sit. If you are early, you will get a choice of seats. If you are late, you get stuck sitting wherever there is an empty chair. It may not be at a table with anyone you desire to meet.

If you are often kept waiting by a family member, friend, or business associate, speak to that person about it. If you don't confront this issue of lateness, she will continue to be late. You will become frustrated and aggravated by her behavior, and you will resent the lack of consideration for your time. You can also schedule the meeting with the habitually late person fifteen minutes to a half-hour earlier than you really want or need her to arrive. This usually doesn't work for long because after the first couple of times, she knows what you are doing and then arrives even later. Explain to your habitually late colleague that you will be leaving at a certain time and if she is not ready to go at that time, you will have no other alternative except to leave her behind. After you leave the latecomer a couple of times, she will get the message you mean what you say and understand you will not allow anyone to make you late.

Overcoming the Fear

One of the most prevalent fears among business people today is attending an event where they don't know anyone. If you find this is a problem for you, focus on the benefits of doing it. In her book, *Path of Empowerment*, Barbara Marcinak says, "Your power ends where your fear begins." Events provide each one of us with an opportunity to meet and develop relationships with potential clients and potential resources. They give us exposure in the marketplace and allow us to practice our communication skills. Networking events afford us the opportunity to create an image for ourselves, as well as give us exposure to people who will potentially become lifetime friends and/or partners.

Sherial Bratcher, an American living in Canada, decided to move back to the United States after the events of September 11, 2001. Feeling there were many opportunities in Las Vegas, Nevada, she moved to this city, not knowing anyone. She joined several organizations, attended many events, and developed numerous relationships. She attended lots of mixers, but felt something was missing . . . people weren't "mixing." People were attending, but they weren't really meeting each other or feeling comfortable with the experience. She had an idea that would guarantee attendees would meet and talk with 15 to 30 other professionals. She also believed networking could be done on a bigger scale in a relaxed business setting where people could feel connected. She felt they should have an opportunity to listen to a speaker and have a learning experience in addition to leaving the event with two or three tips they could put to use in both their business and personal lives immediately. Sherial acted on her ideas and started her business, Diamond Star Events, offering all this and more. Today, Diamond Star Events holds five networking events per week and has an attendance of anywhere from 65 to 350 people at each event.

Sherial partners with her members to create a networking path that helps them maximize their potential. She has achieved recognition in the community in a very short time because of her networking skills and her willingness to help others succeed.

People approach approachable people

Dr. Ludwig Von Bertalanffy, one of the most important theoretical biologists of the first half of the 19th century, concluded we all see images at the rate of 72,000 images per minute and at that rate, when we walk into a room full of strangers, we are automatically attracted to the person most like us. If this is true for us, then it is true for everyone else in the room as well. We can attract others simply by creating the right appearance.

In order to attract the most successful and positive people in the room, wear a positive and successful look on your face and a sparkle in your eyes. Dress professionally and stand up straight. Wear your confidence in your posture and your demeanor. When another person looks at you, smile your best smile and say, "Hello." This will let others know you are approachable.

Self-introductions

Self-introductions are easier than most people think. You tell the other person your name and something about yourself that establishes a commonality with that person.

You will introduce yourself in different ways, depending upon the event and the person you are meeting. Think about where you are. What do you have in common with another person that would bring you both to the same meeting or event?

Basically, we are introducing ourselves to let the other person know who we are and give her an experience of us. We want to make the experience a pleasant one. Look at the other person, offer your hand, if you can do so easily, and speak clearly. Make a brief comment or two about yourself. You might disclose something positive about yourself or something good that has happened in your life recently. You can add a "branding" line if you like. A branding line is a short description that tells people who you are and what you do. It establishes your niche or area of expertise. You might tell your company name and what you do there.

Your introduction should take no more than ten seconds. Ask questions about the other person. Show a real interest in what he or she has to say. People will remember you if you make them feel important.

Business cards

A business card should be designed to introduce you in a legitimate way, giving the person to whom you are introduced a way to remember you and a method by which to contact you.

Have your cards accessible for easy exchange. Nothing interrupts a conversation more than someone digging through pockets, wallets, or handbags trying to sort out where their cards might be located. Always be sure to have a separate place for your own cards so they don't get mixed in with the ones you receive.

When handing a business card to another person, be sure the card is face up and turned toward the other person for easy reading. If he or she doesn't offer you a card, ask for it. As soon as possible, without being conspicuous, make a note on the back of the card that will remind you who she is, where you met her or the name of the event and what you talked about.

Keep the remainder of your box of business cards in your car. Often people we meet say they left their cards back at the office or they just "ran out." If your cards are in your car, you can always dash quickly out to the car to get more. Put a colored card at a spot in the box to remind you when it's time to reorder. Make sure you know how long your printer will take to complete your order and allow enough time to receive the cards before you run out. Check the box regularly, especially if you have an important event on the calendar. You never want to run out of business cards.

When bringing your clothes home from the dry cleaners, slip a couple of cards in the jacket pockets as you hang the clothes in your closet. Put a few cards in your wallet and into each of your handbags. Be sure to include your evening bags. Your cards should be easily accessible at all times.

Remember not to eat finger foods and hand out business cards at the same time. A greasy food-stained card doesn't leave a good impression.

Make handing out business cards a habit. Give out a minimum of twenty-five cards a day and you will have more business than you can handle.

Follow-up

After the event, follow-up right away by sending a note stating it was a pleasure to meet the person and refer to something about which you spoke. Don't solicit business in this note. Don't include a brochure or sales information, unless you were specifically asked to do so. Simply make it a short, kind note that reminds the person who you are and of your meeting. This will make you stand out, as most people don't send hand-written notes anymore.

From time to time, send the person something of interest in the mail. An article on the subject about which you spoke, along with your card, will show you paid attention to her interests. If you read something in the newspaper about that person, cut it out along with the name of the newspaper, date, and page number, and send her a copy. Everyone appreciates having an extra copy of an article in which she was featured.

Don't let a lot of time lapse without keeping in contact. What is the sense in meeting a person if you take so long to contact her that she doesn't remember who you are?

Frankness

Be sure to let people know when you are looking for something, what you are looking for, and if you need any assistance. Do it in a way that allows them to respond comfortably. When people help you out, let them know the progress and the outcome of their efforts. Be sure to thank them for any help in a timely and appropriate manner. Reciprocate as soon as possible.

Remembering names

Isn't it aggravating to run into someone you know you've met before, but you can't remember the person's name? It's probably not that you don't remember the name, but you didn't actually hear the name in the first place.

When meeting someone, be sure you hear the name. Repeat what you heard so you assure the other person you've heard the name correctly. This will give the person the opportunity to correct the mistake right away if you didn't hear it accurately. If you don't feel you heard the name clear enough to repeat it, then ask her to tell you again. If you still don't catch it, ask the person how it is spelled. Focus on the person when you are repeating her name. Listen to her voice as well as her words. Make mental notes of anything that will help you remember her, including her approximate age, features, posture, and coloring.

Anchor the name in your mind by making a connection that will come to mind when you meet again. Think of someone you know or have heard of with the same name, make up a rhyme using the name, or make a connection with something. I help people remember my last name (Moreo) by telling them to think of Oreo® cookies with an "m" in front and to remember that I am a "smart cookie." They always laugh. Some people think it's silly, but they do remember my name.

Be sure to use the person's name during conversation and again when saying goodbye. At the end of the day, write down the names of the new people you met that day along with the date, event, and whatever connection you used assisting yourself in remembering them. As with affirmations, the act of cursive writing makes an imprint on the subconscious mind. This is an excellent memory technique which may seem like a lot of work at first. Once you get in the habit of writing this information down daily, you will automatically do it without thinking about it, and the benefits of remembering the person's name when you need it will be well worth the effort.

Small talk

You should be prepared to engage in small talk. You may have to start a conversation with someone who was, until now, a stranger. If you are prepared, you won't be caught speechless, or just the opposite, monopolizing the conversation talking about yourself. Either of these leaves you both feeling uncomfortable. Have at least three subjects you can talk about with anyone you meet. These could be current events, sports, or local happenings. Being prepared will enable you to have a pleasant exchange and make others feel more comfortable.

You can always comment on the place where the event is happening, the food, or the organization putting on the event. Or you can ask a question about the guest of honor, the speaker, or the event itself. Whatever you do, don't make negative comments about anyone or anything . . . not even the traffic, the parking, or the weather. You don't want to be seen as negative or as someone who finds faults.

Be careful not to spend the entire time at the event talking to only one person or you will not fulfill your purpose in networking. It is appropriate to spend no more than ten minutes talking to any one person. The idea is to circulate and meet as many people as possible. Although it is much easier to latch onto one person for the entire event, it is not nearly as productive.

Many of us stay in a conversation because we don't know how to end it. If you are the one speaking, just continue on with, "It has been terrific meeting you and talking with you. I look forward to our next meeting," and move quickly to another part of the room. If someone else latches on to you, politely excuse yourself. Say something like, "Excuse me, I see someone I've been hoping to catch up with. I've enjoyed talking with you." Or if the conversation was less than stimulating, maybe even downright annoying, say something more along the lines of, "It's been interesting talking with you," and move on. Speak to another person right away so the person you have just left can see you had someone to speak to and not that you simply left him or her because the conversation was boring. Knowing how to end a conversation is as important as knowing how to begin one.

Going with a Friend

If you go to a meeting with a friend or business associate, don't stay so close to each other that it looks as though you are stuck together with Velcro. Go your separate ways, meet new people, then introduce your friend to the people you meet and have her do the same for you. The two of you can have lunch with each other another day. This time is for networking. When you have a plan and go your separate ways, you can double the number of contacts you make. You can also devise a signal to give each other, in the event one of you needs to be rescued from some boring person who has you cornered in an endless conversation.

Joining others

Don't be afraid to join into a conversation that is already underway, but don't be intrusive. Sit or stand close to the group and make facial expressions that say you are listening. You may nod in agreement. When you feel you have been included, then you are free to join into the conversation. You will know by the body language or the facial expressions and eye contact of the others whether you have been included or not.

If you are in a group and you notice someone who appears to want to be included, for goodness sake, include her.

Recently, I attended a professional meeting and several women were talking about restaurants that could be utilized for a future event. Gloria, a very charming and gracious lady, was sitting nearby and heard the word "restaurant," but didn't hear "meeting room," so she mentioned that she had discovered a charming new restaurant and then started to describe it. One of the women from the original group asked abruptly, "Do they have meeting space there? I've been there and I didn't think they had a separate room for luncheon meetings." When Gloria said she didn't realize what the other group was talking about, the other woman explained they had been talking about finding a restaurant where they could hold meetings. Needless to say, Gloria was hurt and embarrassed, which could have been avoided if she had listened to the ongoing conversation before jumping in. The other woman could have been more sensitive to the situation and used a warmer tone of voice. This, too, may have alleviated the hurt and embarrassment. It is always correct to be kind and gracious, even when we need to explain a situation or clarify information.

Name tags

Many people don't like to wear name tags at events. Remember, name tags are provided for a reason. They are supplied so you can address people by their names. In some cases, they also provide other information, such as their job titles or where they live.

I appreciate name tags because sometimes I see people who look familiar and I can check their names before speaking to them, assuring myself they are who I think they are.

Name tags should be worn a few inches below the right shoulder. This way, when you shake hands, the name tag is in the other person's line of sight. If your name tag is worn on the left side, the person must shift her eyes to read it, making it obvious she doesn't remember you.

When there aren't name tags

If you state your name when greeting another person, more often than not, she will do the same. Stating your name saves her the embarrassment of having to ask if she has forgotten who you are.

If you recognize the person's face, but can't remember her name, say so. Don't try to pretend you know who you are talking to when you don't. This could get you in trouble. We are all human and forget a name now and then. If we haven't seen someone in a long time, it's possible she has changed so much you won't recognize her.

When it's time to leave

When you are ready to leave, say goodbye to the people with whom you are involved in conversation and then seek out the host or hostess to thank. Don't make it a long conversation. Just say something as simple as, "Thank you for including me in such a lovely event," and then go. If your host is involved in a conversation with someone else, stand to the side for a minute or two until he acknowledges you are there and say, "Excuse me, I'm leaving now and want to thank you for a lovely evening," and go. Don't hang around waiting for someone to encourage you to stay. Once you've said you are going, go!

If there is no official host or hostess, remember someone has worked long and hard to put the event together. Take a minute to find that person and say, "Thank you."

Mentors

A mentor is a person who has more experience than you and is willing to help and guide you in your development. In many cases, mentors can open doors for you and introduce you to people you may want or need to know. They don't charge fees and they usually have nothing to gain by helping you other than their own personal satisfaction.

The word "mentor" came from Homer's poem, "The Odyssey." Mentor was the teacher and overseer of Telemachus, who was Odysseus' son. Odysseus was the King of Ithaca. When he went to fight in the Trojan War, he entrusted the care of his kingdom to Mentor. Mentor has now come to mean "a trusted guide or advisor."

Most times you will acquire your mentor through work. It may be your boss or a respected executive within your organization. When you ask someone to be your mentor, let the person know why you have asked her in particular. Tell her what you hope to learn from her and discuss how much of a time commitment it might take on her part. In addition, tell her what you can contribute to the relationship. Don't ask someone who hardly knows you to be your mentor. Mentoring relationships are usually built over time. Some organizations attempt to assign mentors to others. These relationships may work in some instances, but in most, they don't. The practice of a speaking group I joined was to assign a mentor to new members. When I received the name of my mentor, I sought her out and introduced myself. She looked at me and said, "Don't expect me to help you be successful. I'm building my own career." I felt like I had been slapped in the face. I have acquired many wonderful mentors in my life. When I joined Soroptimist International, I met several wonderful women who were successful and powerful. I volunteered to be wherever they were. If they were taking Christmas presents to a girls' reform school at the other end of the state, I offered to drive. I thought of all those hours I would have them "captured" in my car. If they were going to visit a Senior Citizen Center, I offered to bake cookies and serve food. If they were raising money for a scholarship for women, I made sure I raised as much, if not more, than anyone else. I wanted them to see me as someone who made things happen. As a result, these five women became some of my best life-long friends.

Early in our relationships, a couple of the ladies invited me to go to lunch and shopping. I was quite delighted. When we got to the store, one woman suggested I make some changes in my wardrobe, my hair, my makeup, and my overall image. Because I respected her opinion, I followed her advice. It was effective. These changes made a difference in how people saw me. Others began to see me as a serious business person instead of a "fashion plate." That was more than 30 years ago. This woman, Lois Sagel, is still my wardrobe consultant today. She selects suits and accessories she knows are my style and support my professional image. Then she calls me to come and try them on. She makes sure the items I buy this year mix and match with the items I have purchased in previous years. The quality and style of the clothing she selects is classic and timeless, so it is appropriate for most any occasion and will look good for several years. I don't mind paying more because my cost per wearing is actually lower than with a lesser-quality item.

Many people come up to me after presentations and ask me to mentor them. It usually is not even a reasonable request, because they don't want to be speakers, they don't live in the same city, and they have no idea of the commitment involved in a mentoring relationship. I usually suggest they find someone closer to home and in their own industry. This is not to say that I haven't mentored people. I have.

None of the people whom I have mentored have asked me to be their mentor. In some cases, I didn't even know I had mentored them until they told me years later about what they had learned from me. In other situations, it was a natural progression of the relationship. One example is Fiona, my business and writing partner. When I first met Fiona, she offered to drive me to some presentations, as I was new to South Africa and she knew her way around. Each time she drove me to a presentation, she sat in the back of the room and listened. On the way home from the presentation, she would ask questions about why I used certain examples, how I put together a presentation, and where I got ideas for exercises. After many of these trips, she said, "I would like to do some speaking, too." I suggested she join Toastmasters International, which she did. She attended the meetings, worked through the manuals and practiced diligently. In a very short time, she achieved her Competent Toastmaster designation and I started making small amounts of time available in my presentations to bring her up to the stage and give her an opportunity to speak. At one Toastmasters event, when I knew she was ready, I reached over, picked up her notes and tore them up just as she was being introduced. This forced her to speak from her heart, since she couldn't use notes she didn't have! She has a wonderful life story and a charismatic speaking style. In that moment her speaking career began.

Another young woman I mentored lives in another state. After I had done a training program for her company, she invited me to join her for lunch the following day. She explained that she had read a couple of my books, had a training background and wanted to write a book of her own.

She then asked if I could give her the names of some resources she needed. I did. Now I continue to send her information as I acquire it and when I am in her city, I always call and invite her for lunch and check on her progress.

These types of relationships are good for both parties. If you want to be a mentor, by all means, do so. If there is some way you can help someone or be a positive influence in someone's life, you will gain a great deal of self-satisfaction in doing it.

Role models

Role models are people you may or may not know personally. It's possible they aren't even alive anymore. They are people who have demonstrated in their lives that they possess or possessed qualities we would like to emulate. They have often played leadership roles. A person can have many role models. Each role model has demonstrated something we would like to learn or some behavior we would like to imitate. They may be people who have gone through challenges, difficulties, or adversity. We admire the way they got through and past whatever it was they had to deal with. Role models can be older or younger than we are. Age is not a factor.

When my cousin, Marla, was going through difficult times in her life, she would always stop and say, "What would Aunt Daisy do?" and she would then consider what Aunt Daisy might have done or said to her, even though Aunt Daisy had long since passed away. Aunt Daisy was a good role model to many because of everything she had experienced, survived, sacrificed, and accomplished. Most importantly, through it all she exhibited love. We always knew she was there for us.

Coaches

Life coaches help people improve the quality of their lives. Unlike mentors, they charge a fee for their services. They spend a certain amount of time with you in exchange for a certain amount of money. They are trained to listen, observe, and assist you in finding strategies and solutions. A coach is there to provide support for you. Many of us don't have a support system and a good coach can make a positive difference in our lives by helping us to hone our skills, improve our performance, discover our creativity, find resources, and enhance the overall quality of our lives.

If you don't have someone in your life who can do these things for you, I recommend you hire a coach for yourself. If you can't afford it, find a way to do so. You may be able to trade services with your coach, work a second job, or save any discretionary income so you can afford a coach. It's important to have an impartial and knowledgeable third party who can advise you and help you achieve your goals.

Associate with positive people

Associating with negative people who have no initiative will pull you down. If you want to be successful, you must go where successful people go, do what successful people do, and cultivate friendships with people who have goals and ambitions. Talk with people who not only have big dreams and big ambitions, but people who make things happen and have made things happen. Lots of people talk a good story, but when it comes down to getting things done, what do they do? What have they achieved? What are they accomplishing now? If your goal is to be a leader, associate with leaders. Emulate the qualities and behaviors of those people and you will soon find that you are a leader, too.

My dad always said, "If you associate with the best, you will become one of the best." Choose your friends and associates for their values and qualities. Don't leave your associations to chance.

Associate for Success Exercise

Attend a function this week that you don't normally attend. Go by yourself. Make a plan for what you will achieve at this function. In this plan be sure to include: What you will wear, what kind of contacts you will make, who you want to meet, the minimum number of people to whom you will introduce yourself, how you will introduce yourself, how many cards you will give out, how many you will collect, as well as how and when you will follow up.

When you return to your office or your home, write down whether or not you worked your plan and achieved your goals. If you did, congratulate yourself! If not, analyze and write down why you didn't accomplish what you set out to do.

Whether you did or didn't achieve your goals this time, pick another function and repeat the process. Continue to do this until you have built a successful network.

_____

_____

_____

_____

_____

_____

_____

_____

_____

_____

_____

_____

_____

_____

_____

_____

_____

_____

_____

_____

_____

_____

_____

_____

_____

Association Affirmation

My life is rich and full. I am surrounded by love and support. I attract positive, powerful people who believe in my success. I meet the right people at the right time. People like me. I am more than enough.

Chapter Eleven

Overcome Life's Obstacles

All changes, even the most longed for, have their melancholy;
for what we have behind us is part of ourselves;
we must die to one life before we can enter into another.

— **ANATOLE FRANCE,** NOVELIST
AND **NOBEL PRIZE** WINNER

Have you ever thought to yourself, "There are days when I wish things were like they used to be. I wish I could go back to a time when I felt safe and secure. Sometimes I wish change would slow down. I just start to feel comfortable with my life and something else happens, changes, or goes wrong. When is it ever going to stop?"

Most successful people believe things happen for a reason. What are the reasons for what has happened in *your* life? Acknowledge it, but don't dwell on it. Examine what you have learned from it and then get back to concentrating on the future. When we stay "future-focused," we bounce back quickly because we are taking control of our lives and maintaining our self-esteem.

Unexpected circumstances

My friend, Debbie, was driving her car in Johannesburg in the early evening hours. She had the window slightly cracked open so she could enjoy the brisk, fresh air. When she stopped at a red light, a young man stuck his hand through the window, pulled up the lock release, which also released the locks on all the other doors. As quick as a flash, he and three other young men jumped in the car. One of them put a knife to Debbie's throat and told her to drive. Fearing for her life, she did as she was told. They took her to Alexandra Township where they stripped her, raped her numerous times, and cut her with large machete-type knives. When she confided her experience to me, she said she didn't know how many of them raped her, but there were many. In between the rapes they taunted her, forced her to commit degrading acts, and sliced her skin with the knives.

When they decided they were finished with the torture and humiliation, they told her to run for her life. They said they were going to count to 100 and then chase her down, catch her, and kill her. She was naked and bleeding, but luckily, she was in good physical shape. She ran through dark streets in a ghetto far worse than any we have in America. She asked people to help her to no avail. They said they were afraid if they helped her, the boys would kill them. She ran until, exhausted, she came upon an old man sitting in front of a hut made of tin. She fell to her knees and begged him for help. He told her there was an old car in the yard behind the school down the block. He instructed her to crawl into the trunk of the car and not even peek out until he told her to get out. She did as instructed. She really had no other choice as she had no idea where she was and she was too exhausted to run any more. Debbie told me later it seemed like hours she was in the trunk of that car. Finally, she felt the car moving slowly. She just curled up in a ball and prayed the person driving was someone who would do her no more harm.

Eventually, the car stopped and the trunk opened. The elderly, gray-haired man helped her out and drove away. He had driven her to a police station in a Johannesburg suburb and left her there in front of the station, naked and bleeding. She walked into the station where they wrapped her in a blanket and called her father to come and get her.

Dealing with the trauma

A few months later, she realized she was very angry. She felt she needed an outlet to express her anger. She went into an artist supply store and bought a canvas, a brush, and some paints. She had never painted before, but she felt like she had to do something to express her rage. It made her feel much better. When she had finished three paintings, she took them to a shop to get them framed. To her surprise, the proprietor of the shop asked if he could buy them. She said, "No." He then asked if she could do more paintings like them, which she did, continuing to dump her rage as she painted. All of the subsequent paintings were sold. Today she has paintings hanging in galleries throughout southern Africa.

Take back control

Debbie is so thankful to that wonderful man who risked his life to save hers . . . a total stranger, whom she had never seen before and most likely will never see again. She prays he knows how much he means to her. At the time it happened, she was in such shock she didn't even get his name or tell him how very much she appreciated the risk he took. Two years have passed and Debbie still has to have regular HIV tests and continue this practice for a long time. But she has taken control of her life. She still has nightmares and bad days, but she is focusing forward and making a new and better life for herself. In truth, she acknowledged her feelings. One of the things she realized was that she blamed herself for not rolling the window up all the way. Would that have prevented this horrific experience? No one will ever know. It's in the past now. She had to learn from it, forgive herself, and turn her anger into a productive outlet that helped her to heal on a spiritual level.

Gaining a new perspective

Reinterpretation of the negative events in your life gives you power. Remember, our thoughts create our feelings, which influence our behavior. So, if we reinterpret the event, we change our behavior. If you tell yourself you are a victim, you will feel like a victim, behave like a victim and people will see you as a victim. If you are focusing forward and thinking of the possibilities, you will feel positive and behave in a positive manner. You will be seen as a person in control of your life. People who are in control are definitely not victims. If you do the positive things, you are not only a survivor, you will heighten your belief in yourself and strengthen your determination to succeed. You begin to live again with new *purpose*, new *passion*, and new *power*.

This is not easy. It's hard — very hard. Life's problems, challenges, and obstacles come to all of us in different ways. You must decide whether you will use these setbacks as an excuse for not being successful and not having the life you want, or whether you will become more determined to live the rest of your life the way you know you should.

Hardships are a gap between where you are and where you want to be. Obstacles can be opportunities in disguise. When you can find opportunity even through your fear and pain, you can transform your life.

A better tomorrow

My business partner, Fiona, was a young married woman with two babies when Rhodesia, the country where she was born and lived all of her life, came under the power of a radical communist leader and became Zimbabwe overnight. She and her husband feared for their lives and the lives of their boys, but they had foreseen this moment and had been preparing for the change.

Over a period of three years, they built a 56-foot ocean-going vessel, storing canned food and other necessary living supplies in the hull of the ship as they built it. When the right moment came, they took the boys and drove across the border towing the ship, as if they were going on a holiday. They left their home and all but a few of their belongings behind forever. They crossed the border to a new country and a new life. Fiona said the scariest moment of her life was when the customs officials searched the boat and vehicle for anything they deemed to be contraband. They breathed a sigh of relief once they were across the border, even though they had great sadness at leaving the life they had always known.

Adjustments and consequences

Adjusting to a new life in a new country with all the hardships and very little money led Fiona and her husband to divorce. Fiona got a part-time job working mornings and took her babies to work with her. Eventually, she moved into a full-time position and was able to hire a woman to look after her children. She went back to school at night in order to educate herself further and move into increasingly better positions. She began working in sales, because she knew sales would provide the opportunity to determine her income. In the twenty years I have known Fiona, I have watched her persistence and determination to succeed take her from salesperson to sales manager, from managing director to vice president and ultimately to owner of various companies. Her commitment to life-long learning has given her an advantage over others with higher degrees from more prestigious schools. Today, she is writing books and giving others the benefit of her education and experience.

Making the choice

Instead of becoming a victim, Fiona chose to take charge of her life, participating purposely and deliberately. Her most recent victory has been to survive cancer. She applied the same steps to overcoming cancer that she applied to the difficult situations in her life. Fiona's steps were to carefully and realistically evaluate the situation she was in, determine her goals and write them down, be actively involved in making positive changes, take action, even though she was afraid, and never give up. Everyone can use Fiona's steps to better themselves and overcome the obstacles life may put in their way.

Fiona once told me, "Life is a do-it-yourself project, just like building a house. You can carefully and lovingly build it with the right material and it will require very little maintenance, or you can erect it sloppily with inferior materials and watch it fall apart. You build a quality life by taking one step at a time until you've overcome your obstacles."

Life's obstacles

These two women, my friends Debbie and Fiona, were given extreme challenges to conquer. They used their knowledge, skills, and courage to create stepping stones to their new lives. They epitomize the words of an old poem that says,

> *To each is given a shapeless mass,*
>
> *A book of rules and a bag of tools,*
>
> *And each must fashion, ere life has flown,*
>
> *A stumbling block or a stepping stone.*

These are extraordinary examples of women who took what could have been stumbling blocks and instead, fashioned new lives for themselves and their families. It's possible the challenges you and I encounter aren't as difficult as these. It's also possible you have been through changes or experiences that were every bit as challenging or even more difficult.

Life is not always easy. Life is either getting better or worse. We are getting better or worse. Nothing stays the same. If we work at being just one percent better every day, we will have a much better life. Even a slight change now can mean huge changes for you down the road. Imagine a ship leaving Southern California set for Hawaii. If the ship sails just five degrees off course at the beginning of its journey, the ship could sail right past its destination. If you determine where you are headed and intentionally focus on that goal, you will sail straight toward it. You have to learn to adjust your course when you encounter a storm, and never lose sight of where you are headed.

Dealing with change

How we handle change is determined by our reaction to change. We can attempt to ignore change, hope it goes away, and take no action toward making anything better; we can be reactive and attempt to cope with the consequences of change once they have happened; or we can choose to be proactive and prepare for the change, so we can take control of it when it happens.

In order to take control of change, we need to determine who or what is creating it. We need to understand how this change is going to affect us. We need to consider what specific issues will have to be dealt with as a result of the change, how we will cope with them and most importantly, what opportunities change will present. Change always brings opportunities with it.

The influence of technology

In addition to what happens in our personal circumstances or relationships, we live in a time where technology is constantly changing our lives. Dr. Robert Hilliard, Chief of the Educational Broadcasting Branch of the Federal Communications Commission pointed out, "At the rate at which knowledge is growing, by the time a child born today graduates from college, the amount of knowledge in the world will be four times as great. By the time the same child is 50 years old, it will be 32 times as great and 97 percent of everything known in the world will have been learned since the time the child was born."

What this means is that change is occurring at an ever-increasing speed. Technology was supposed to make our lives easier, but in fact, has made our lives more difficult. It's changed the speed with which we communicate. Everything is hurry up, learn more, be more, and do more. We stretch ourselves so thin that we don't take the time to enjoy life. We take our computers on vacation, talk on cell phones in the bathroom, and conduct business at every hour of the day and night. We spend hours stuck in traffic, eating breakfast and text messaging our children, spouses, and offices all at the same time. We don't make time to take care of our bodies, because of the demands placed on us. We don't go to lunch; we eat at our desks. We don't have dinner with the family, because we are all in separate rooms watching different television shows.

Global Factors

Competition in business is greater than ever before because of the reach technology affords us. We can do business in the global market without even leaving our offices or homes. At the same time, people can find out almost anything about us without our permission or knowledge. They can even steal our identities.

Additionally, the volatile world situation has given us a sense of insecurity and to some degree, a loss of freedom. For those of us who travel a great deal, we must add two to three hours to our itinerary to get checked in and through security at the airport. We hope there is a food concession open if our plane is delayed. We hope there is a shop open at our destination so we can buy makeup, hairspray, and other liquid or gel toiletries. It's no wonder we become more stressed and our patience wears out quickly. Whether traveling for business or pleasure, we experience the frustration and anxiety of dealing with our feelings about the world situation and the changes it has forced upon us.

Uncertainty and perspective

All in all, everything is more uncertain. Your perspective will determine how this uncertainty affects you. You can perceive it as a threat of some kind and be resistant to it. You can openly disagree with it, or you can whine about it and try to manipulate it. You can even pretend it isn't happening.

Or you can perceive it as inevitable and look for the opportunity for growth that the change offers you. Of course, there will be times when you feel uncertain or out of your comfort zone as you deal with change. The process may be uncomfortable. Eventually the change becomes the norm. It becomes the new, better way and you'll wonder why you ever resisted the change in the first place. You have now expanded your comfort zone.

Change can be good

Helene told me how she hated dealing with change, right up until the first time she used a fax machine. Twenty years earlier, she had used TWX/Teletype, an office machine you might see in an old movie or an antique shop. It was awkward, huge, and time-consuming to use. She feared the new fax machine coming to her office would be similar.

The sales representative delivered the machine and showed everyone how to use it, by punching in the fax number of another office and sliding a paper into the appropriate slot. That was it. It was as simple as dialing the phone. Helene remembers asking, "That's it? You mean I just enter this number and my order is instantly received across town, or maybe even across the country?" She continued, "You mean that by using this machine, I no longer have to get in my car and drive an hour each way to deliver a document?" She was amazed at its efficiency and time-saving benefits. She couldn't believe she had been afraid of this miraculous machine, which, as you know, is as easy to operate as a telephone. Helene vowed never to resist change again. Change can be a good thing — a very good thing!

Making a friend of change

John Naisbitt said in his book, *Megatrends*, "If we can learn to make uncertainty our friend, we can achieve more than in stable eras."

Most Americans change careers three times in their working lives. So if you have lost your job, rather than saying, "I'm unemployed," why not say, "I'm exploring opportunities." After all, that is what you are doing, isn't it? Optimism is a choice. You can even add a positive comment, like

"I'm very excited about my possibilities." You create your own power. You supply your own positive energy and your motivation to move forward. No one else can do this for you.

I love the story of the baseball umpire who was asked if the pitch was a ball or a strike and he replied, "It ain't nothin' until I say what it is." Well, that's exactly what's happening with you. It ain't nothin' until you say what it is. You can call your game as you choose — success or failure.

What's next

If you are at a point in your life where you feel you have failed or that life has dealt you a losing hand, you might want to remember the words to the Kenny Rogers hit recording, *The Gambler.* "You have to know when to hold 'em, know when to fold 'em, know when to walk away and know when to run."

It may be time to fold 'em, walk away, or even run. In order for you to survive, you may need to do something that doesn't involve the past. My friend, Fiona, walked away from everything in her life that was familiar because she saw the dreaded changes coming her way. Her ability to embrace a new, unknown future with courage and determination has brought her many rewards, both financial and spiritual. My friend, Debbie, literally had to run for her life. She chose to turn her tragedy into a productive way to heal herself and make a living.

Letting go of what doesn't work

Sometimes, you have to "fold 'em;" know when to quit and move on to whatever else you want to do. Deepak Chopra, doctor and author, talks about the dangers of staying in a job you find unrewarding, unsatisfying or unimportant. He tells us of the harm we do to ourselves when we choose to trek off each day to a job we hate, because we are too scared or pessimistic to pursue our true passion. Our bodies will manifest symptoms in an attempt to get our attention!

The Woman's Heart Foundation states: "Studies show the most common time for a heart attack to occur is Monday morning." The BBC reported, "The stress of returning to work on a Monday morning can trigger a dangerous increase in blood pressure." They went on to say, "The Tokyo Women's Medical University study shows blood pressure readings are higher on Monday morning than at any other time of the week. It may explain why deaths from heart attacks and strokes tend to peak on a Monday morning. There are 20 percent more heart attacks on Monday than on any other day."

A matter of life and death

When you consider these statistics, you will realize you have an obligation to pursue your passion and move forward, focused on your goals and dreams. It can literally mean death to stay in a situation that makes you unhappy. I'm not saying you should quit your job with nowhere to go, but if you devise an exit strategy and are careful and thoughtful, you should be able to make the necessary changes. Where would you like to go?

Life is a gamble. Change happens and we are the ones who must deal with it. It's how you play your cards that matters. There will be stress, uneasiness, uncertainty, and doubt. You can choose how you will handle it. Will you cling to your fear and remain in the same old game just because it's comfortable or familiar? Or will you ante up for a new hand and face change as a challenge and an opportunity, thinking of it as an exciting adventure and use your self-reliance and self-confidence to take you to interesting new places? Will you welcome change as a growth experience and empower yourself? Will you keep your eye on the goal and reward yourself when you reach your destination?

Assessing the situation

Take a good, hard look at yourself and ask yourself what you are going to do. Do you understand the rules? Do you have the tools? Do you have the talent, the skills, the knowledge, and the contacts to make it work? If not, how can you get them? Start making a plan.

No life experience should be wasted. From everything you have done or experienced, you have gained knowledge. You have gained skills and grown as a person. You have learned new things to do. You have learned what not to do. You can use all of this knowledge to carve out a new future.

Christopher Hegarty, a business advisor and author, once told me, "In twenty years, you will be the same person you are today except for the people you meet, the experiences you have and the books you read."

You'll be amazed at what happens to your life when you deliberately set out to meet positive people, have new experiences, and read good books. I started attending more and more seminars, networking events, and business functions. I made myself talk to people I didn't know, even people who intimidated me. In a short time, meeting new people no longer intimidated me. Once I determined to make it about them and not about me, I was more comfortable. Don't try to impress people. Instead, show interest in them. Find out who they are, what their thoughts are and what experiences they have had. You'll gain so much by being interested in others. Your mind will expand in new and different directions and opportunities will begin to present themselves.

You never know where your next idea will come from, so be open to learning from everyone. Make it a point to get value out of every encounter.

Rising above the problem

The next time you are faced with an obstacle, try to deal with it in a positive manner. Even though you may think it will be challenging to overcome the obstacle you are faced with, decide to embrace the stumbling block and turn it into a stepping stone instead. I could write a long list of friends and associates who were devastated when they lost their jobs or got laid off. Others lost their homes and businesses in recent hurricanes. Ultimately, every one of them managed not only to survive, but to thrive as a result of the challenge. You've probably even heard someone say, "Getting fired was the best thing that ever happened to me."

Getting more by letting go

Lisa opened her own public relations firm after being dismissed from her job. She now employs more than fifteen full-time workers and represents entertainers, restaurants, and businesses. She is hugely successful.

Carolyn quit her job to start her own public relations company. Las Vegas was still growing in leaps and bounds and there was room for everyone. She had only three thousand dollars in her bank account the day she quit her job. Anyone who has ever started a business knows three thousand dollars is not a lot of money for a start-up. Aside from paying your overhead on the new business, you need to buy everything from business cards to office furniture and equipment. In addition, you still have your living expenses to pay. Carolyn was very brave to take such a drastic step. She did it because her job had become a stumbling block on the road to her dreams.

Susan knew what she wanted and was future-focused. She wanted to get married, have kids, yet still work and have an income. She was working for a casino hotel and spent most of her time taking care of emergencies and employee problems. She was working anywhere from sixty to seventy hours a week. The property where she worked was a huge corporation. Do you think a corporation cares if you ever have enough time to start a family? Of course not! They have a business to run! Susan saw her situation and the futility of it. She saw how her job didn't mesh with her other life or career goals, so she made the necessary changes. What happened to her? She now owns one of the largest events management companies in the state, employs twenty people and recently bought her own office building. Not long after she launched her new business with her new husband, she called to share a high point with me — her former employer had hired her firm to handle a special event for them! Can you imagine how gratifying that was for her? Since then, that same company has used her company's services many times. She is excellent at what she does, knows her business, and believes in herself enough to follow her heart. She took that big stumbling block and turned it into an amazing opportunity.

Stepping up

When you know where you are headed, the stumbling blocks will, in effect, become stepping stones. Learn to embrace the challenges you face. When you look back at some of the major challenging events in your own life and see how you were able to handle them effectively, you can see how you grew from those experiences. Now, look back at any challenging situations you were not able to handle well. Do you think you can do better now? Of course you can! We are all growing and learning constantly. When you believe life's obstacles present themselves for a reason, you will be better able to overcome them.

Overcoming Obstacles Exercise

Make a list of the obstacles you have encountered in your life. Give yourself a gold star for each one you have overcome.

1. _____

   _____

2. _____

   _____

3. _____

   _____

4. _____

   _____

5. _____

   _____

6. _____

   _____

7. _____

   _____

Overcoming Obstacles Affirmation

I believe in me. I know I am strong, capable, and creative. I release the past and stride confidently toward my future. I speak words of praise and encouragement to my inner self and watch with pride as my life unfolds with success. My future is mine to create. I am more than enough!

Chapter Twelve

Achieve Power Through Faith

Close the door of fear behind you and see how quickly the door to faith will open in front of you.

— NAPOLEON HILL
AUTHOR, *THINK & GROW RICH*

Things do work out for the best. If we are to survive and be happy with our lives, we need to believe that. We need to have faith that things will go as we want them to, that we will be safe, that we will have clothing and shelter, and yes, even as Scarlet O'Hara said in the classic movie, *Gone with the Wind*, "After all, tomorrow is another day."

What is Faith?

Faith is the confident assurance that something we believe is true or something we desire is going to happen. It is the absolute certainty that what we hope for is waiting for us, even though there is no tangible proof.

In today's stressful world, people have a greater need for spirituality than ever before. We need to know there is a reason and a purpose for our lives. We also have a need to know we aren't floundering about on our own. We must absolutely understand and know in our hearts there is a power in the universe bigger than we are. This power is with us and for us and gives us strength in good times and bad. It is always supporting, comforting, challenging, guiding, and loving us. Those without faith feel lost, empty, and alone — and the sad part is they don't even know why they feel that way.

Faith is a very personal thing

This power is whatever it means to you. Many of us have different names for this power. How you sense, feel, and communicate with this power is your personal choice. Many of us believe as we do because we were born into our faith or we were taught as children to believe in a certain doctrine or religion. Many of us have been taught there is only one way to believe and to be faithful. I believe there are many paths to a spiritual awakening. I choose to call the power in my life, "God." This is what I was taught and what I am comfortable believing. I also believe that whatever you call this power, whether it is Creator, Buddha, Creative Intelligence, Spirit, or Cosmic Consciousness, a higher power is there for everyone. Once you **accept** that there is a higher power and find your own expression of your faith, you will be amazed at what your belief will do for your confidence. This belief in a higher power gives us the strength to get through the tough times. It gives us the courage to face change and step out into new adventures. Courage is the willingness to maintain our faith, even in the face of all contradictions.

Count your blessings

Whenever we find ourselves resisting our life circumstances, rather than reacting out of fear, anger, or despair, we can choose positive actions to get us out of undesirable circumstances. Whenever we wonder if the positive experiences we want in our lives will ever come about, we must stay focused on the good that is already present in our lives and be thankful for the blessings we have.

When Sharon's son was born, the doctor told her that due to a heart problem, her son would not live beyond the age of two. She and her husband had a solid faith in God and an unwavering belief that their son would survive. They celebrated and gave thanks for every day of his life. Instead of accepting a death sentence, they held faith and built a future. Their son is now 25 years old.

When you choose to live anchored in faith instead of thinking about what you lack and your limitations, you will feel calmer and more peaceful. You will be better able to think clearly and find solutions to problems, make the right decisions, and choose the right path for your life, instead of running around in a frenzy grabbing anything and everything that looks like an easy answer. Any time you act out of fear, you give up your power. Kim Kiyosaki states in her book, *Rich Woman*, "While fear can warn us of life-threatening events, it can also be a killer — a killer of dreams, of opportunities, of our own personal growth and passion, of living life to its absolute fullest." When you choose faith instead, you will have more control over your life and more power to make things happen.

Ask and listen for the answer

Kate was supposed to have a meeting after work, but forgot the papers she needed for her meeting, so she drove home to get them. It was August and hot, so when she got home she went into the kitchen to get a drink, but no water came out of the faucet. She went on to her meeting, and while driving back home, she was thinking about not having any water and wondering what to do. She asked out loud, "God, what am I to do?" That's when she heard a voice that said, "Call Thelma." Thelma is a partner in a water drilling company. So Kate called her and said, "I've got a problem. No, I've got two problems. I don't have any water and I don't have any money." Thelma replied, "Well, we can definitely help you with the first and we'll work on the second." Thelma sent one of the crew members out to check on the water problem and found the pump needed to be replaced. By the next day, Kate had a new pump and was able to pay for it in installments. In addition, the drilling company offered her a better paying job than the one she had, so she went to work in their office.

Most people want a better life, whatever they believe that may be. For some it might be a bigger and better house or money in the bank, while for others it could be good health or more leisure time. It is not selfish to seek the best for you and for your family. It is only selfish when we want to keep it from others. We were meant to do great things, to have happy and prosperous lives. Learn to make your requests known with thanksgiving and acceptance.

God's answer, not yours

I've talked to God my entire life. My mother was a very spiritual person. She knew her Bible backwards and forwards. She knew the life stories of all the people in the Bible, as well as who was related to whom. She told us these wonderful stories with enthusiasm and kept us fascinated for hours. She taught us that good begets good. She cleaned us up and took us to Sunday school and church. Afterwards, we'd discuss the lesson we heard that day. We prayed together as a family at night. She taught us not to be prejudiced against people of other colors or other faiths. And most of all, she taught us it was more important to demonstrate our faith than to talk about it.

As a teenager, I prayed God would take care of my family and make things happen the way I wanted them to happen. I tried to make bargains with God that if he would give me what I wanted, I wouldn't smoke or take my brother's car and race it on the country roads.

As I grew older, I continued going to church every Sunday, praying every night and believing that all I had to do was go to church, pray, and be kind to other people and everything would be perfect. But life happened anyway. My sister was in an accident where the car rolled over her arm and crushed the bone; my dad died; my brother lost his legs in a motorcycle accident; my niece died in a boating accident, and my nephew's motorcycle accident destroyed his face, blinded him, and left him in severe pain for the rest of his life. In addition, my marriage failed and I divorced. So many things failed to go according to my plan that I began to wonder where God was, why He let things happen the way they did, why He was not making life happen the way I believed it should. After all, I was a good person.

Touched by spirit

One day I was driving to visit my Mom at her home in southern Utah. I had just returned the day before from Africa; it was a very long flight and I was exhausted. A small animal ran in front of my truck and I swerved to miss it. When I did, I lost control of the vehicle and the next thing I knew the truck was rolling end-to-end. Everything seemed to be in slow motion and I remember thinking, "It's okay to die now because I am right with everyone." Then I heard a voice say, "No, it's not time yet." I don't know if I heard it inside or outside of my head, but I heard it loud and clear.

At that same moment, I saw a wispy cloud of white air. It seemed to cover me and hold me. The truck continued to roll and I could see pieces of the metal breaking off and flying past. When it stopped rolling, I crawled out of the truck and up the embankment to the road. There were big piec-es of glass and metal on the road. I started pulling the debris to the side of the road, so no one would hit it when they came around the curve. My truck was upside down and my personal belongings were literally scat-tered over the hillside.

It was a while before anyone drove by. At last some boys found me wandering along the road and called 911. An ambulance took me to the hospital in the nearest town and as we rode along, the young attendant picked glass off my face and out of my eyelashes with tweezers. When they examined me at the hospital, I had a dislocated shoulder and was in shock. Other than those minor things, I wasn't hurt. Considering how much glass had shattered in my hair, on my face, and on my clothes, it was surprising there wasn't even a scratch on me.

When I told my mother about the experience later, she said, "The Holy Spirit covered you and protected you." I believed her then and I still be-lieve that is what happened to me that day.

Conscious connection

In spite of this dramatic episode, there were still times when I didn't always feel connected.

Then I realized it was not God who had separated from me, but me who had separated from God. I was still saying my prayers every night, but I wasn't saying them with belief or faith. I was saying the words, but I wasn't listening for the answers. Instead of trying to get God to fix my problems, I started asking God to help me find the answers, use my knowledge, and understand how to create harmony in my life and the lives of others.

Once I resumed inviting Him into my daily life ... to my speeches, programs, conferences, and training rooms, as well as acknowledging His presence in my home and in my heart, and asking Him to touch the hearts of the people in my audience, my connection grew strong again.

There are no limitations placed on us by God. We are the ones who put limitations on ourselves. We are supposed to live constructively with purpose, passion, and power. We were born to be happy and creative, to enjoy life and prosper to the fullest. We are the ones who set ourselves up for failure and unhappiness. When we do this, it is usually done subconsciously. We aren't even aware that the actions we are taking are self-defeating! We must constantly concentrate on what we are becoming.

Imagine if Nelson Mandela, the first black president of South Africa, had given up on becoming what he has become. South Africa would never have become the "one man, one vote" free nation that it is today.

If we take time daily to sense the presence of God in our lives, faith takes hold and the chance of something new and wonderful will be more likely to happen. We will go from fear to faith, from aloneness to connectedness, from lack to abundance and happiness.

Law of nature

A power greater than us, God, has created many systems. Everything in the universe follows an orderly course. Whether it's the seasons, the planets, or our lives, there's a system. You've heard it said "What you sow, so shall you reap." In other words, what we think, say, and do comes back to us. Since this is true, then shouldn't we be more concerned with what we give than what we get? Shouldn't we show people we love them and care about them without being overly concerned if they love us or care about us? Shouldn't we make sure the words which come out of our mouths say what we really believe?

Surely we are intelligent enough to realize that our environment responds to our mental state. We will always be experiencing the effect of our thoughts and actions. We create our own limitations. If we say we are too old, then we are too old. If we say we are too fat, then we are too fat. If we say we are too stupid, then we are too stupid. If we think and say negative things long enough, our subconscious will eventually believe these things and act on them. Whatever the negative thought is has to be changed if we are to change the effect it has on our lives. We must learn to bless our lives instead, and be grateful for what we have, even when we feel that what we have is not much. To find fault with ourselves is really finding fault with our creator and that doesn't make sense. We are each perfect in our own way. We must not look at our mistakes or bad habits as flaws, but think of them as opportunities to grow.

Look for a new option

If you find yourself in an undesirable situation, don't spend too much time belaboring how you got there. Instead, think about how to get out and get to where you want to be. Sit down and make a list of the options you have. There are always options — no matter what circumstances you might be in. You might have lost a promotion, only to find the person you deemed the least qualified got that job! Worst of all, that person could become your boss!

You can choose to plan some kind of revenge, decide to become a lousy employee, or you can create another option. You can choose to change your attitude and cooperate with that person, or you might even choose to leave and go to work somewhere else. It's possible that the result of what was originally perceived as a negative event could actually force you to take action. It might be exactly what you needed to make the necessary changes that could result in your being in the position to move up to a higher level than you ever imagined. You could even put yourself in a place where you could become the CEO of a company in a very short time.

People who spend all their time thinking about what is wrong almost never discover the joy of living. They fail to see that there is potential in every event, no matter how negative or wrong it may seem at the time.

We must come to realize we are not destined to fail or have sickness and unhappiness. Sure, many things are not right in this world and many things need to be changed. We can make these changes as long as we work with the laws of nature, rather than against them.

Eliminating Fear

Actually, the only thing we should be concerned with is fear. We can deal with circumstances around us. It is the lack of confidence in God that should be cause for concern. The power of God is with us. When we give up fear and hate, we will come to understand the unity of life. We are all connected to each other. Our cells are regenerated and renewed by the air we breathe. This is the same air that someone near us just exhaled. By virtue of the fact that we breathe each other's air, it is easy to see how connected we become.

Do you ever cry over something that happened to someone you don't even know? You might be watching the evening news as a reporter talks to someone who just experienced a devastating fire, an earthquake, or some equally devastating loss and you find yourself in tears. Why? Because we are all connected! As much as you may want to deny it or think you can't be a part of someone you don't like, we are joined by our biological makeup and our spirituality.

Anxiety about our affairs indicates belief . . . the wrong kind. You are afraid, and therefore, believe things will not work out. You either have fear or you have faith. You can't have both at the same time. Doubt is a belief. You are choosing to believe the negative instead of the positive. When you wish things will work out for the best, but you aren't sure they will, then you are living in hope, not in faith.

Why do we project the blame for our limitations upon God? It is not God who limits us. It is our ignorance of the consciousness which God has given us. We need to boost ourselves up to greater wisdom, guidance, and self-expression. If you will take the time every day to sense the presence of God, you will pass from fear into faith. Start today by giving yourself permission to have faith and belief in order to achieve the things you want to achieve.

Working with Faith

Don't misunderstand. Faith by itself is not the answer to all that is wrong. While we rely on faith for guidance and comfort, it is our actions that produce the results. We must act on the love and the peace that comes from being connected to God. We can sit on a mountaintop and contemplate God and believe in our success in life, but unless we go out and take the steps that are necessary, nothing happens.

There's a story you may have heard about a man whose home was flooded by the overflowing of a nearby river. The water level was so high that the man's house was completely under water, except for the roof. Believing God would save him, the man crawled up to the roof and waited. A man standing on high ground threw him a rope and said, "Grab hold." The man on the roof said, "No thanks. God will save me." Some other men came by in a rowboat and said, "Jump in," and the man on the roof said, "No, go ahead. God will save me." Then a police helicopter came by and offered to pick him up and, again he said, "No, go ahead. God will save me." The water rose above the roof, and the man drowned. When he got to heaven, he asked God, "Why didn't you save me?" God replied, "I sent you a rope, a boat, and a helicopter. Any one of those would have saved you. Why weren't you willing to do your part?"

You have to take what God offers you and use it to your best advantage, even when things are not going the way you had planned. As tough as this may be to understand, there is always a reason for the adversities and challenges in our lives. You don't always have to spew forth religious platitudes, what you know, or what you have learned. Sometimes what you know is for your own knowledge and gives you the confidence to do the things you need to do. Demonstrate what you believe by your actions, as well as your words. Your actions make the difference between what you have, what you don't have, and how you influence others.

Sharing of self

Did you ever write a check to contribute to a relief effort? Why would you care? You probably think, "If a disaster like that ever happened to me, I hope and pray someone would help me." We must care about each other. It's easy when the people in need are family, or people we know from our community. It's a greater challenge when they are in another part of the country or the other side of the world.

We all know people who go to church and quote their religious beliefs incessantly. Yet these people have tons of clothes they can't wear or haven't worn for years which they are hoarding in the back of their closets, instead of packing them up and giving them to someone in need. There are people who have enough stuff in their garage to furnish another house, but instead of helping someone else have a more pleasing place to live, they hoard their stuff in boxes in case they might need or want it someday. Some people even rent storage units in which to keep all their old stuff, instead of sharing it with a needy family. These are the same people who gossip, condemn others' behavior, and talk negatively about their own lives and the lives of others. Many of us know people who use their religion as an excuse for judging or hurting others who are different from themselves. True belief doesn't leave room for judgment and it doesn't neglect or hurt others.

Invisible proof

There are other people who believe what they can't physically see is not real. They might as well say the ocean isn't there, because they've never been to California. Science has proven time and again that there are many things we can't see … such as electricity, gas, sound waves, winds, and gravity. We don't see these things, but they certainly do impact our lives. And so it is with God. Just because you can't see Him or prove his existence, doesn't mean He isn't there. More than thirty studies have found a connection between spiritual or religious commitment and longer life. One of the most extensive reviews demonstrates the connections between religion and health cut across age, gender, cultural, and geographic boundaries. In an article in Reader's Digest, October 1999, Dr. Dale A. Matthews, Associate Professor of Medicine at Georgetown University Medical Center in Washington, DC states, "We cannot prove scientifically that God heals, but I believe we can prove that belief in God has a beneficial effect. There is little doubt that healthy religious faith and practices can help people get better."

Choose Faith

We can wake up today and choose to have faith, just like we can choose to start a diet, be happy, or change any other habit. We can begin to live a new life any day we choose. It doesn't mean our old lives go away. It means we've started down a new path. Just like staying on a diet isn't easy, having faith isn't always going to be easy. We have to be committed to it. We have to work at it every day. Just like any other journey we may take, we're going to hit dead ends and take detours. We may even run out of gas. But we are the ones who make the choice to complete the journey or give up.

When we fail, it's because we prepared to fail. We thought about it, we believed it could happen, and then it did. When we put our trust in God, we talk success, confidence, and belief. We talk faith. That is when we succeed.

When life happens

My mother married when she was right out of high school. She married the man of her dreams and had two beautiful little girls. She was pregnant again when her husband was killed. Two weeks later, she gave birth to twins. She now had four children, no husband, no money, and a high school education. What was she to do? She moved back home with her parents and got a job as a seamstress working in the home of the woman across the street. She paid her mother to watch the babies, running home to see them during whatever breaks she could get. Her mother constantly told her to give her children up for adoption, as she certainly couldn't afford to keep them. My mother was adamant that she would never give up her children. She didn't believe God gave them to her for her to give them up. She would take care of them, love them, protect them, and make a good life for them. She saved what money she could and eventually she got a place of her own for her family, and hired someone to watch the children. For four years, she worked as the housekeeper at a hospital. Then World War II erupted, which provided women greater opportunities for employment, as men marched off to war. Mom looked in the newspaper for a better paying job and saw a classified ad for a mechanical draftsman. As my mother had always been a good artist, she applied for the job. The ad said to "bring your portfolio." She took pictures she had drawn of people, animals and objects. The woman who interviewed her sent her home to draw pictures of nuts, bolts, and screws and bring them back the next day. Mother sat up all night drawing those pictures to scale. The next day she was hired and sent to school to become the first mechanical draftswoman that aircraft company had ever hired. She went on to become a member of the design team that designed several of the aircraft used in World War II. After two years, this mother of four married a man she had met at the hospital years ago, and a year later, I was born. My mother's faith never wavered. She always said God was with us, loved us, and protected us. During those challenging years, though times were tough and money was scarce, her faith was strong.

Whenever I had doubts about my abilities or whether or not I could have something or go somewhere, my mom would always say, "Have faith." And then she would say, "Draw a picture. If it doesn't start looking like you want it to, erase it and start over." I knew that meant if I wanted something to happen, I had to do something. I had to believe and take action. I'd cry, "But Mom what if I do the wrong thing?" She'd say, "You'll never know if it's wrong or not, unless you try."

William James, the father of modern psychology in America, believed, "It is the faith that we have in advance of a doubtful undertaking that is what assures its successful conclusion."

Remember, thoughts are how we create our lives. What we think about, we bring about.

Follow life's rhythm

Since God created us in his likeness, this means our minds are in the likeness of His mind. Our intelligence is in the likeness of His intelligence. God's mind creates and so our minds create. Therefore, it makes sense that our minds are either a part of God's mind or are directly linked to it. This means that by thinking, we can set "the law of God" into action in our lives.

Man doesn't create his power of thought. He uses it. He can use it either in the right way or the wrong way. God's truth and God's laws are always with us. It is up to us to recognize and use this power to bring good into our lives and the lives of those around us, as well as the world at large.

As I mentioned before, there is a system and a rhythm to the universe. It's God's rhythm. Day follows night. Night follows day. First comes winter, followed by spring, then summer and autumn. Then we return to winter. It is our job to get into the rhythm of the universe. God wants us to achieve, to have what we want, and to live a good life. It is up to us to remember and accept that fact.

God's law is always working

Even when we appear to be failing, God's law is working, because the law says "as we believe, we receive." When you believe you will fail — you will. You are putting the law into motion to work its truth and then proving it is true.

There is a poem my mom used to recite to me when I was a child that illustrates this point so well:

> *I bargained with Life for a penny,*
> *And Life would pay no more,*

However, I begged at evening
When I counted my scanty store.

For Life is a just employer,
He gives you what you ask,
But, once you have set the wages,
Why, you must bear the task.

I worked for a menial's hire,
Only to learn, dismayed,
That any wage I had asked of Life,
Life would have willing paid.

Cause and effect

The law of *cause and effect* tells us we can change the effect only by changing the cause. If we are thinking negative thoughts, we are going to get negative results. When you keep doing the same old thing in the same old way and you expect to get different results, it's not only called insanity — it's called pure stubbornness. If you want different results or a different effect, you must change the cause or the original thought.

Once you understand and accept this, it will change your life. You can no longer blame outside forces or other people. You must recognize you have the power to produce either results of success or results of failure within yourself. Faith will bring you whichever you choose. Negative faith will bring you negative results. Positive faith will bring you positive results. The choice is yours. As this sinks in, the shock may be startling. Each one of us is completely responsible for what happens in our lives.

Everyday Faith

As we live our lives, we experience various degrees of consciousness. Whatever we have experienced thus far might have been experienced differently, if only we had understood that our expectations produced the results we achieved. If you want to grow strawberries, don't plant turnip seeds. If you want love in your life, don't plant hate.

Faith is not something we practice only when things are not going the way we want or expect. Practicing faith when we are miserable and discontent, because we figure that we'd better "use" God now to make things better, is not really having faith. It is exploitation. Faith should be practiced at all times. God is here for you. He is the light that guides you and gives you strength and courage during the good times and the bad.

We make choices every moment of every day. When we choose to trust God, take part in creating our own destiny, show gratitude for the progress we've already made and stay forward-focused, we will see miracles at every turn. Then and only then are we moving toward a future filled with unlimited possibilities.

Faith is the confident assurance that something we believe is true or something we desire is going to happen. I am absolutely certain what you hope for is waiting for you.

Strengthening Your Faith Exercise

Write a letter to God. Express your appreciation for all of the gifts and talents you've been given. Remember to be grateful for your challenges and the lessons learned from them. Share your honest feelings about your life thus far. It's okay to express your angers, fears, and frustrations. This letter is not to ask Him to fix your problems, but rather to acknowledge that He will give you the courage, the confidence, and the strength to do what must be done for a positive outcome.

When you have finished, put it in a sealed envelope with the date on it. A year from now, take it out. Read it and see how your life has changed, and if you feel differently than when you wrote the letter.

Building Faith Affirmation

God is my source. God is my supply. I am cherished and blessed. All that I am, all that I do is supported and sustained by the gentle hand of God. I am worthy of His love. I am more than enough.

A Final Thought . . .

Remember when we talked about your dream? It is now time to focus on turning that dream into a concrete goal. If you were taking a trip, you wouldn't walk up to the ticket agent at the airport and say, "I'd like to buy a ticket" without having some idea of where you wanted to go. So look at your goal as your life ticket to a wonderful journey.

You never want to look back on your life and say, "I wish I had done it differently." You may have heard the expression, "People don't plan to fail. They simply fail to plan." If you don't have a plan, then you are indeed planning to fail.

Once you have the plan, you must take action. A plan without action is not going to bring any success. It is shocking to know that with all the information and opportunities available to help us become successful today, so many people are only getting by. Don't let that happen to you.

Expose yourself to opportunities. Being in the right place at the right time is often a matter of planning properly and working your plan. Associate with people who have done what you want to do. Associate with people who are headed where you want to go.

We learn behaviors and habits from the people we are around. It's important for you to spend time with successful people.

Go after what you want with passion! Success is as competitive as any sport. Don't sit back and wait for someone to discover you. Get out there. Do something. Don't underestimate yourself and overestimate others. You have as much ability and brain power as anyone else, if not more. You are not inferior to anyone. Turn off any negative or doubtful voices in your head and listen only to the sound of the little train, "I think I can." Stand out while fitting in. Staying within the realm of acceptable behavior, set yourself apart from the crowd. Put all your effort into what you do. Do more than is required. Do it to the best of your ability.

Life is a succession of choices. You have the ability to choose. Choose **purpose**. Choose **passion**. Choose **power**. **You are more than enough**.

About the Author

Judi Moreo is a performance enhancement specialist whose unique approach to helping people succeed has made her one of the most sought-after keynote speakers in the nation at corporate seminars, leadership conferences, and conventions.

As an executive in South Africa during times of turmoil and unrest, Judi learned firsthand what it takes to be successful amidst political, social, and cultural upheaval. Today, she lives in Las Vegas, Nevada, and serves as president of Turning Point International, a performance improvement company that operates in the United States and South Africa, and was awarded a "Circle of Excellence" Award by the Las Vegas Chamber of Commerce. Her client list reads like a who's who of the world's most prestigious companies and organizations.

Judi served on the boards of directors of the Las Vegas Chamber of Commerce Women's Council, the Las Vegas Professional Speakers Association, the World Modeling Association, the International Association of Model Agents, and Women in Communication. She received the "Outstanding Achievement and Community Service Award" from the American Women in Radio and Television, was honored as "Woman of Achievement — Entrepreneur" by the Las Vegas Chamber of Commerce, and was named "Nevada Business Person of the Year" in 2003 by the U.S. Business Advisory Council.

Judi also publishes a monthly e-zine, *Motivational Tidbits*, which shares success stories of others. If you would like to receive this complimentary e-zine, share your story and help others benefit from your growth, or would like more information about Judi Moreo's broad range of services, including speaking, training, consulting, and published materials (CDs, tapes, and DVDs), please visit her website at www.judimoreo.com or contact:

Turning Point International
P.O. Box 231360, Las Vegas, Nevada 89105, phone (702) 896-2228
You may purchase the companion book, *Goal Achievement Journal* in bookstores everywhere and online.